Volume 1

Harmony
with Horses

Beginning Your Horsemanship
the Right Way

Leslie Hodgson

Illustrations by: Kelly Boccia www.kellysboccia.com
Photographs of Leslie and Gold Digger by: Michael Holton
All other Photographs Noted
Additional Photos on Cover by:
Benjamin Cook www.designingbuzz.com

Dedicated to my three little girls:
Starlynn, Launa, and Harmony
I thought my heart was full when I was a
kid loving horses and then again when I
met your father, but you three girls have
expounded my heart in more ways than I
can explain. Sharing the love of horses with
you has been some of the most meaningful
and rewarding experiences of my life.
I love you all!

TABLE OF CONTENTS

Harmony with Horses

Harmony with horses can happen in small ways every day you are around them, if you seek it. If you seek it, there will be times you just adore everything about them, and in turn, they love and respect you. This is harmony. There will be times in your riding where everything feels "right". That is harmony. Times will come when everything about your day feels full of purpose because you have a responsibility for your horse's happiness. When your horse feels and radiates that love and dedication you have for him, and seeks to show it back to you... that, my friends, is harmony.

Webster's dictionary describes harmony as an accord or agreement. An accord or agreement is when two different people, or things, settle on the SAME thing together. Since the term "harmony" is most commonly used in music, we will use music examples to explore the word 'harmony' further.

Picture a piano. It has many different keys, white and black, and each makes its own sound. If you have ever played the piano or have seen it being played, you will know that you use two hands, with each finger playing different keys. You will also know that some keys played together make very beautiful sounds, called "chords", and some keys played together make a rather unpleasant sound.

Melody is different than harmony. Melody is just ONE line of notes in a song, played with one hand, and one note at a time. But, to play with all sorts of different notes, you need HARMONY. Harmony is the other lines of the song, different notes, played with different fingers on different keys. When the right notes are played together, it sounds like ONE sound, not several different sounds sounding at the same time. Again, this sound of unity and oneness can only be made when the right notes are played together. This is what harmony is: two different parts sounding as one. The two different parts are identical in every way, except for being separated by several steps.

Harmony can be achieved when riding a horse in much the same way as playing a song. We need to become identical in every way even though we are "separated" by the differences in our anatomy and natures.

Achieving harmony with horses is a constant quest because it requires improving your horsemanship day after day. Having great horsemanship is a very rewarding trait.

Each person has probably been exposed to horses a little bit differently. Most likely though, anyone who loves horses probably shares a mutual feeling toward the animal. Their beauty and strength can entrance you. You feel excited to be around them. They interest you greatly... how do they see the world? You feel a need to help them be comfortable and happy. You wish you could talk to them... to let them know how you feel towards them. You want to sit on their backs and fly over a mountain together. You want to show the horse that as a team, you can enjoy the highest levels of success, whatever success means to you.

These feelings are the core of true horsemanship. If you have feelings like these towards the horse, you are on your way to actually achieving all of these things.

Taking an active role in horsemanship has just landed you the title of athlete and artist. You have the opportunity with the horse to create art... to express your love of the horse to the world. Only through correct technical application and through your passion and dedication to the horse will your attempts be truly art.

To have CORRECT horsemanship, we must build a strong foundation. An architectural building that stands the test of time has done so because it has deep rooted foundations, built of strong materials and by craftsman who took the time to make sure it was done right.

Make sure you do not rush through this book or the first

few years of your riding career. Make sure you slow down and do it right. It takes years for any athlete to be physically and mentally strong enough to feel they are ready to go to the world championships or the Olympics or for any artist to be pleased enough with his work that he feels he has something to share with the world.

So again, don't rush. Don't get discouraged or frustrated. Know that it takes time. Luckily, every time you are on a horse it is fun! So, even if it is taking time to master a certain concept, you are on an animal that is powerful and majestic and that you enjoy being around!

This will be a book that you should refer back to all through your riding career. You should work on your form and communication with the horse any time you are around them, always trying to improve yourself and them day after day.

Get as much instruction as you can, practice as often as you can and read and watch any materials that will deepen your knowledge and understanding of the horse and correct riding techniques.

Horses Are In My Heart In Everything I Do
Leslie's Story

Horses are in my heart in everything I do. The feelings I have for them have been there for as long as I can remember. I remember holding a small model horse in my hands when I was about 6 years old. I would stare at it, just letting my eyes run over it again and again... starting at the face, up and down the arch of the neck, and over its back, noticing the lines that made its muscle structure. I marveled at the beauty.

I decided then that I wanted horses to be in my life... as much as possible. Being a "horse-crazy girl" was an understatement as my parents can tell you. I lived and breathed horses. I asked if I could start riding horses with my mom and older sister, and soon, I was on their backs, learning, and loving it. I listened to everything my instructors said, because I wanted to be good at riding horses.

Besides just the time I had at the barn, horses were continuously part of who I was. Every project at school that allowed for some imagination and creativity, I incorporated horses into it. Model horses crowded my room, along with my horse wall-paper and lamp. I had a bracelet made of my horse's hair.

I was somewhat serious about the whole thing, and most people that know me say that I still am. I took competition seriously, always wanting to do my best. When I went in my first lead-line class, my two horse trainers had other girls to take in, and my mom was going to take me. I kept asking if one of my trainers could take me in, and finally, my mom got fed-up and asked why I didn't want her to take me in. I said, "Because mom, you are really good at thirds".

We all laugh about that to this day. Though, it was a serious issue to me back then. In the lead-line class, everybody got a blue ribbon, but they called my number fifth (because they called us according to our numbers.) So, I told everybody I got fifth. I was ok with it... I just wanted to try and do better next time.

When I was about 12 I had next door neighbors that had their own ponies as well. Everyday after school, we would get cookies and milk and then go tack up our ponies. The three of us were anything we wanted to be... the Pony Express, Cowboys and

Indians, Professional Show Jumpers, or Vaulters (yes we did tricks and stood up on our horses). We also had a club house that we would tie our ponies up to and let them rest and graze. Michelle and Pixie, Nicole and Shaker, and myself and Squirt... we were quite the group! Michelle also had a big grey appendix-quarter horse named Ghost that we would do our vaulting on. We fox hunted together, went to summer horse camp together, and had frequent sleep-overs that included midnight moon-rides on our ponies. Those ponies will be blessed in heaven for being such angels to us. Our days would be long and fun and often, our parents had to peel us off our ponies so they could rest, and we could eat dinner.

Through the years and still now, horses grow deeper and deeper rooted into who I am and how I live my life. They have taught me amazing life lessons. I love a challenge, and horses and riding challenge me everyday. They teach me patience, love and long-suffering. They teach me how to be brave, and overcome my fears. They teach me that dedication, persistence, and passion can create an image and a feeling so beautiful, that is it hard to put into words.

Together with horses, I have won many awards. Together with horses, I have made it through difficult times in my life because of the quiet comfort they provide. Most important to me, is the opportunity, and the blessing I have had to share this magic with others.

Horses provide an opportunity for all to overcome mental and physical barriers within themselves. Horses are used for pleasure, competition, and some are used as therapy horses, for many different patients. Horses can have a healing nature. You will find they can heal you as well, if you know how to open your heart and find it.

EQUIVENTURES started because of the magic I found in my partnerships with the horses, and also the magic I found between horses and kids. I was a kid when I began my affinity with horses, and I know how important they can be in the lives of such a horse-crazy kid. Having such a large, majestic, though very dependant animal creates a feeling of responsibility in a person. Having that feeling of responsibility to and love for the horse has proven to keep many kids grounded to their principles.

The main objective of this manual is to teach people to love the horse unconditionally. If you love the horse, truly LOVE the animal and care for his well-being, everything else in your horsemanship will fall into place. You will give yourself the opportunity to become the best rider and handler you can be.

Every aspect, principle and technical teaching in this book is taught for those who care. They are all taught to give avenue for your true feelings to be made manifest to the world.

Have fun reading it. Do not rush through. A strong foundation stands the test of time, so build one for yourself—strong and true to the core.

My horse:
Gold Digger V

Gold Digger V

The "model horse" for this book is my beautiful Arabian mare, Gold Digger V. She was bred by, in my opinion, the top breeder in the Arabian industry, Sheila Varian. Sheila and her partner, Don Severa, leased a mare named AM Gloriana Bey (Bey Oro x Khemosabi daughter) and bred her to their stallion, Desperado V.

We bought Gold Digger before Sheila's Summer Spectacular Weekend in the year of 2000. Gold Digger was in Washington, where I live, with a local trainer ... and we bought her before she was to go back to California for the Summer Spectacular. We still went that year, and the whole three days I was known as the girl who bought Gold Digger. Some were disappointed because they wanted her, but all offered their congratulations and support.

Gold Digger is a very unique Arabian. There are not very many that reach the height of 15.3 hands high... but she does. And she reaches it in the most elegant, beautiful way. If Gold Digger was a human, she would be a super model. She has perfectly straight, long and angled legs. Her neck is long and archy, perfectly proportioned to her body, and set on it is a gorgeous dishy face... perfectly chiseled. Her eyes are large and dark, and her beauty captivates me everyday. Honestly, every day when I look at her, I fall in love all over again.

Her motion is probably her best physical trait. She floats as if on air. What makes it even more incredible to watch, is that she knows she is beautiful, because I and others tell her all the time. When she has an audience, or feels particularly beautiful, she is as fancy as can be.

What I enjoy more than that, is the times we have alone. She gives her attention, her talent and her spirit to me, and practically begs me to ask her to do something she can prove herself in. Sometimes, she thinks she knows what I am going to ask her, and she'll do it herself, so I have to keep each workout fresh and different.

Gold Digger is known by all as the princess. She is true to her name... quite the attitude she has!! Some take it offensively, but I just smile, knowing that a horse with that much personality makes life interesting and fun. I can relate to Gold Digger in many ways. I don't let her get cranky or bossy with me, and she respects me for it. I respect her for always stating her opinion and letting me know what she thinks of each situation.

Working is what she loves to do best... even more than turn out, and even more than getting her itchy spots scratched. She is always willing and ready to work and show. She would probably go all day long if I asked her to. I have met my match in attitude and ambition.

-Written in 2003, Leslie age 20.

Section 1

Our Equine Friend
Understanding Horses

Gemstone LC (Blackstone Bey x Takara Padrona) Photo by designingbuzz.com

Wondrous Generosity

Student Ariana leading Bey Anna Shah+/ after thier lesson. Photo by Leslie Hodgson.

Horses throughout history have consistently served us, even when it was taxing on their body and spirit. We owe them our heart-felt gratitude.

Horses were the second animal to be domesticated by man (dogs being the first). Humans found horses to be useful, and soon they were loved as part of the family. Arabian Horses in the Arabian Desert became so loved that they slept inside their master's tents. Indians loved and protected their horses as well.

Horses began to spread across the world, and were soon used for transportation, farm work, mill work and anything else we needed their strength for. Horses even carried their masters into war, braving the elements of whizzing bullets, slashing swords, cannon fire, and death.

However, the horse is not our main way of transportation any more, and the military uses machines to do the transporting and fighting. Horses aren't "needed" as much in everyday society.

Still though, they ARE needed and many people revolve their lives around them: horsemen, horsewomen, breeders, raisers, trainers, and horse crazy kids.

Through all of this, horses have endured much. Even though we asked the horse to perform difficult tasks, they remained loyal and loving to us. Their work, their history and their character is enough to give anybody unbounded adoration for them.

How can something so big and "wild", a "beast of burden" which surely would not have to ever let us touch them if they didn't want to, be so willing to love back as we love them? It's amazing they even let us sit on their backs, let alone jump over fences, climb steep hills, endure long journeys and work the way they do.

SRF Make Myne Mynk++/ in her show days, and now as a very kind lesson horse.

Horses and humans can become such a united partnership that they can compete together AT THE OLYMPICS as ONE—a team. It is marvelous and completely amazing how willing the horse is in all its endeavors. They cooperate and contribute to us in incredible ways. They are incredibly tolerant of having to carry around a "potential predator" on their backs—doing it even when it causes them pain. And day to day our love grows.

Even with all of these great things to be amazed at, there is still the little day-to-day things that can deepen our love for the horse: their nickers when you come in to feed; the submissive acts of lowering their heads for the halter; a child being carefully toted around by a retired show horse; the affectionate nudge on your back when the horse wants attention.

On a different note, it also is amazing how quickly the horse can learn to accept something he is afraid of. When we present something "scary" to him—a trailer to load into lets say—and he gets unsettled, we can gently and assertively get him to remember that we are his trusted leader and he will soon feel assured and obey our requests.

Let yourself experience this with horses. Open your heart and your mind and notice and appreciate what the horse will do for you.

You will notice, as many have noticed, that they not only comply to our requests with gladness, they also look for ways to please us of their own free will.

Horses participate in a two-way partnership. It is a wonderful partnership... a wonderful way of life.

Beginning to
Understand the Horse

The best way to begin to understand the horse is to know what a horse is. A horse is a PREY animal, which means that they get hunted. Horses have to look out for predators all the time which makes them alert and sometimes skittish or jumpy. Domesticated horses have never seen their herd being hunted, however, their instincts are strong and will always be a part of them.

Proof of this is how they spook at unfamiliar sights and sounds. A plastic bag can sound like a predator in a bush getting ready to pounce. A big dog laying motionless in the sunshine is also a subject of suspicion for the horse. It is true even, that a big boulder lying on the ground is scary to some horses, "What if it's a bear?!" your horse will ask you.

The horse's 2 biggest fears as a prey animal:
To Get Eaten
To Be Trapped

Why is it important to understand this about horses? Perhaps the most important reason is that WE are predators. Our species hunts and eats meat. So, let's imagine ourselves as big tigers. We are trying to form a partnership of predator and prey.

We have to convince the horse that we are not out to eat them and that they can rely on us to be their trusted leader. The horse will grow fond of our friendship and respect our leadership.

Always keep in mind that we can easily ruin the trust/ friendship/leadership we build up by lashing out in our anger, or cruelly forcing the horse to do something against its will or nature.

We must learn how, and always keep the precious partnership we have formed pure and reliable.

A Horse's Behavior

A horse behaves the way it does based on these three things: almost everything in its genetic structure; its past experience; and its current environment.

Remember, a horse is a prey animal... they just want to survive. Their instincts are an inseparable part of their natures. You will often see different breeds acting somewhat differently. This also is reflective of their genetic structuring. (Remember though: there are some in every breed.) Their genetic structure means what their parents and ancestors have passed on to them. Different breeds act differently and different "families" within the breeds will act differently. It is just the same as our parents giving us each unique looks and character traits.

A horse's past experiences can affect the way they behave because horses have GREAT memories! A lesson should be learned by this knowledge we have of them to never give them reason to doubt your leardership or destroy your trust. Though many horses are fortunatly forgiving, most emotional wounds made at the hands of humans take ages to heal. Conversely though, a horse's continued good experiences with humans will deepen their trust and willingness to please.

Just as our current environment affects our behavior, so it does with the horse. Do you act differently at Chucky Cheese's than you do at a fancy restaurant? Do you act differently around different groups of friends? Do you respond better to someone that asks you to do something nicely rather than when somebody demands something of you? So does the horse. Their "current environment" is what setting they are in, what mood they are in, what mood their handler/rider is in, their surroundings, and their routine.

The Herd

Horses are a herd animal. This means they like to be together with their own kind. This gives them a sense of safety from the scary world of predators because together, they can always be alert and aware of danger, and are willing to flee and fight together to protect their way of life.

Though a bond can be created between horse and human that the horse will feel comfortable being by himself, any horse, without exception will usually choose to be with other horses. This is simply because of his instincts and nature.

A horse out in a big field with his friends is the most happy horse you will ever see. They get to roam around with their friends munching the day away. Together they chit-chat, squabble over the water bucket groom each other, avoid or pester the herd bully, dash to the other end of the pasture when something scary was seen, doze on the cool grass, and of course roll in the herd scented dirt!!

Horses are predictably more uncomfortable when they are by themselves. They will always feel vulnerable without the added security of other horses. This being said, it is good to know that herd behavior will develop in any group of horses that are together in the pasture, the wild, at shows, in the riding arena, etc.

Horses crave a sense of familiarity and belonging, just like we do! Having a consistent group of friends that they can call their "herd" can fill that need for them.

Herd Structures in the Wild

Instead of ferociously defending his herd from predators as people commonly perceive stallions to do, he is more of a herd-organizer. The stallion always trails the back of the herd when they move on. He keeps them all together. However, the stallion **will** fight when another young stallion comes to try and take over his herd.

The "Lead Mare" is the one who leads the way while the stallion is busy keeping the herd together. The lead mare is the alpha mare, sometimes called the "boss mare". She is the one who makes the decisions in leading the herd to move on to new grounds. Most often, she is also the herd police... the law enforcer. For instance, when a young colt starts to think he is too cool and pays too much attention to the other mares, the lead mare will send him packing with strict reinforcement.

The other mares of the group are the ones who produce the foals or help to take care of the foals. Young fillies sometimes stay with the group when they get older, but most often wander off to join with a group of "bachelor stallions" or to get claimed by another stallion. This is how inbreeding gets avoided.

Young males are driven out of the herd at about 18 months of age because the mature stallion will feel threatened that he will try to take control of his herd and breed his mares. Young colts often join up together, and then as they mature, they will go challenge other established stallions for their herd, or begin to fight each other for the young fillies that joined up with them along the way, to establish their own herd.

In a general herd that you will find in your pasture, if there is enough food to go around, you will rarely see fights. In fact, serious fights are hardly seen in equine living, especially in the wild, because horses enjoy peaceful community living. They desire harmony and try to avoid conflict.

Horse Language

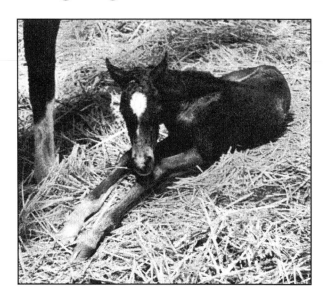

What the horse's communication does best is express their mood, emotional statements, and opinions of their situation and surroundings.

Their language is often very subtle and can only be seen or heard with knowledgeable perceptivity of our own. All horses, no matter breed, size or place of birth, speak the same language.

We can interpret their subtle language clues by the response it gets from other horses, or the action that comes immediately after the language sign. We cannot communicate to the horse as much through smell and taste, but what we see, hear and express with our bodies can be understood by both.

The most important thing to realize about communication is that it is going on CONSTANTLY. Every move we make says something to the horse. Either, "this person is very relaxed and pleased with me", or "this person is uptight and he might attack me soon!".

Horses are obviously very pleased when we understand what they are trying to tell us. Most often they can communicate to us their pain or discomfort, and when we respond, the horse's trust in our leadership and judgment deepens. The horses know we are not that great at picking up on their communication attempts... and thankfully, they will keep trying. When the horses stop trying to communicate is when we have to worry.

Ear Language

Pricked Forward　　Relaxed　　　Moving　　　Pinning

There are many different positions the horse's ears can be in. The different positions can be for hearing, and for telling us or other horses things. This is part of the horse's language and we can learn how to "read" it.

Pricked Forward: This is a "Who Goes There?" attitude. When a horse hears or sees something suspicious, they need to raise their head and use those radars to pick up any sound they can in the direction of the danger or curiosity. You will also notice them put their ears all the way forward when you are holding a treat in front of them or carrying hay towards them as well. They have their whole concentration on the object that they have their ears turned towards.

Relaxed Sideways or towards the back: This is a listening and/or relaxing attitude. While relaxing, the ears in this position can cut out unwanted background noise. Horses can also have their ears like this when they are concentrating internally, say to their own bodies if they don't feel well, or on their work when exercised with clear purpose. Listening ears are ones that are faced in your direction, while on their back, lunging them, leading them, grooming them, etc.

Moving: The ears can act independently from each other. One could be facing forward towards something they are looking at, and the other could be focusing on something to the other side of them, or listening to you on their backs. Horse's ears are always moving. There is a big world out there with a lot going on! It is a world filled with predators, work, other horses, and feeding time!

Pinning: This ear position is a warning sign to offending horses or people. It says, "go away!". It could also be a sign of pain or discomfort. Some horses also pin their ears at their displeasure with getting their girth put on or tightened. With horses like this, take care to do this slowly and with the least amount of squeezing and tugging possible. Don't let your horse be rude about it, but be considerate of them as well.

Other Language Signs

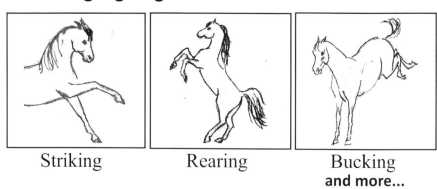

Striking	Rearing	Bucking

and more...

Tail Swishing: This is sometimes a sign of discomfort... but can also be just in response to pressure on his person, or to get away pesky flies.

Tail Clamping: A horse will clamp his tail if he is frightened by a startling noise, or a touch he did not expect, or if he doesn't want that area of his body getting worked with. Also, a clamped tail with his coat standing on end signals that the horse is cold.

Nostril Pinching: When the top part of the nostrils get closer together and looked as if they were "pinched" is mostly a sign of displeasure in something being done to him. The nostrils being pinched could also signal a sign of pain or discomfort some-where on or in them. Look for other signs, and refer to section 4 for more exploration.

Stomping Feet: When a horse stomps his feet, he could be either irritated, impatient or angry. Check for pestering bugs around the horse, or any other cause that could irritate him. For impatient purposes, your horse will just have to get used to the time it takes you to do something, but no horse should be tied up for an obscenely long amount of time.

A **head held high** and a tense body signifies that the horse is on the alert, frightened, and ready to run! This will signal to the rest of the herd that they need to get ready to run too. And it can signal to you that your horse might bolt or shy, so be ready, and handle the situation with understanding and patience.

A **horse's lips** are can also signal what he is feeling through tenseness and looseness.

"Bulging eyes" (open wide and whites sometimes show-ing) is another sign of fear.

A **head held low** means the horse is content and accepting. This horse is approachable by all other horses or humans. There are many different language cues in between the head held at its highest capacity, and the head held low at its most relaxed.

"Licking and chewing" of the mouth is a sign of submission. Unruly colts will get kept at a far distance from the herd by the alpha horse until he shows this sign of submission by turning his body sideways, dropping his head and making motions with his mouth known as "licking and chewing".

Striking, rearing, and bucking are large body signs. Horses use striking for severe warning to "stay away!" Rearing and bucking can be done playfully, as if to say "I feel good!" And can also be used in fear or frustration. Striking is made with a front leg lashing out and usually making contact with the offending object, and is usually accompanied by a squeal. Rearing is when the horse stands up on his hind legs, for short or long periods of time. Bucking is where the hind end lifts into the air and then kick out.

Kicking and biting are defense mechanisms. Horses often kick when something startles them from behind. They also kick when they are angry, in pain, or want something or someone to go away. Kicking can also be done playfully. To other horses it is not such a big deal, but extreme caution should be taken when you turn your horse out to pasture or when you are "playing" with them in paddocks or fields. Especially young horses, who might not have learned that you aren't a horse yet. Biting can be a quick nip, or a full out grabbing of flesh. Horses nip and bite each other to get their way, or to get horses to get out of their way. Horses generally use biting with humans to defend themselves from any danger or pain they are being afflicted with.

Horses that are happy and treated well should have no reason to ever bite or kick in defense, therefore, they won't. Care should be taken to maintain respect from the horse in reminding him that you are not a horse. Nibbling can turn into affectionate biting, so be careful. Some horses kick out when they are let loose, so, watch out! Encourage your horse to get far away from you before performing acrobatic stunts!

| Snort | Neigh or Whinny | Nicker |

Vocal Noises

A **snort** is a forceful exhale out the nostrils. This noise alerts other horses of possible danger and lets them know what direction it is in. It might also serve as a warning to the approaching danger to "keep your distance!"

Horses **neigh or whinny** to let other horses know where they are, or to say, "where are you?" Then, it can also be used in response to say that they heard the other horse. The neigh or whinny is a long call made with the mouth wide open, and is almost always answered by another horse if they can hear. All a neigh or a whinny does is to collect and send information on the location of each other.

A horse's **nicker** is a wonderfully delightful sound. It is low and inviting. It usually says a welcome hello to familiar friends, or is a greeting to a human bearing food! Stallions can use a nicker to woo his ladies, and a mare's nicker to her foal communicates her concern and tells him to get closer to her.

Squealing is not very attractive and is loud and clear. It usually says "watch it" or "stay away from me". This is also a sound used by mares "in season" and ready to be bred.

Cribbing

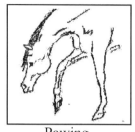
Pawing

Weaving

More Language Signs

Horse's can have "bad habits" that are another form of communication: cribbing, pawing and weaving being the most common.

Cribbing is a quite irritating habit that horses can form. It is when the horse holds something stationary between his teeth and pulls back. There is a characteristic grunt that can be heard when cibbing occurs. Contrary to popular belief, the horses do not "swallow" air. The grunt is made by the sound of the air passing the soft palate as the air rushed by it. Cribbing is a desperate act to fill their stomach. Once a horse has started cribbing, they are highly unlikely to stop, because it is very satisfying to them! Cribbing only causes danger to their teeth, and to the object they are cribbing on.

Pawing is an action the horses do with their front legs, similar to the action of hoeing a garden. Pawing is usually always used to show their eagerness to get to something they are being held back from. Horses also use it to show their frustration at not getting what they want. You will see horses use it to break up their flake of hay so it is easier to eat, dig through the snow to get to the grass they want to eat, or dig a hole in the dirt to try and get water.

Weaving is side to side rocking of the head, shoulders and sometimes even the whole body. Usually, the behavior develops because the horse either went through some mental trauma, or is currently suffering. Some horses just do it in times of excitement, when they want to get fed, or know that it is time to go out and play. Weaving most often happens in the stall, but can also be seen at the pasture gate when they get left behind from their friends, or when they know it is time to come in and eat. The weaving horse is just saying that they want to get going and is irritated with the gate or door in front of them that is holding them back!

The Horse's Senses

Hearing

The horse's ears are like radars. Hearing, along with sight is the horse's main defense system. A horse's hearing is definitely better than our own. Our ears are in a fixed place. Their ears are set high on their heads and have superb mobility around 180 degrees. They can pick up the slightest noise and pinpoint its location, way before we can.

Sounds tell the horse a lot of what they need to know about their world. A rustling bush could mean there is a predator ready to pounce. The sound of the grain bucket means its time to eat! All sounds tell the horse something. We can use this to our advantage. For instance, we know that the horse responds to the tone of our voice. A soft voice can calm them and a harsh voice can scare them.

Horses can get nervous when their ability to hear is restricted. Wind, for example, muffles the sounds they need to hear to survive. So when it is windy, the horses are more on edge.

Sudden noises cause the horse to be startled, especially if they are loud. Remember, a horse's main instinct is to stay alive. They are afraid to be eaten or trapped. Any unfamiliar sound is likely to be both worrying and fascinating to the horse.

Horses do get used to certain sounds, like the sounds of cars, farm machinery, hose filling up the bucket, etc. Though, we must always keep in mind that loud and insistent noises will be stressful to the horse. They feel safe and relaxed in low-level and normal sounding environments.

Horses understand different tones and learn to individualize sounds. They can recognize their friends by their whinnies and neighs. From experience, they can even recognize the sound of individual car engines. They know if it is the tractor coming to clean their stalls, or the car that carries the person that feeds them!

Use the Horse's Hearing Ability in Your Care and Training
Take care to always be respectful of the horse's sensitive hearing. Know how to not startle them, do not blare music, and know that some things might spook them, and be ok with that.

Our voice can be used for many different things. Encouragement, chastisement, to make a request, to give a tactful warning to our approach, provide reassurance in a frightening situation, or simply strengthen the bonds of trust and confidence between us by "talking to them" during our handling and grooming.

Sound is a HUGE part of the horse's life. Remember who and what they are, and don't let their spooking at things offend you. They are just trying to stay safe, and keep you safe as well.

Sight
A horse can see 340 of the 360 degrees around it. The only place it cannot see is directly behind itself, and an area in front of and beneath his muzzle. That is a far larger peripheral field of vision than our own! Their eyes are also double the size of ours.

This vast view is attributed to how large the horses' eyes are and where they are set on its head. They are set more on the side than our eyes are, because they are a hunted animal, and have to watch out for attack from behind.

Our eyes are placed on the front of our heads, and that is what we need as "hunters". We will not stumble as much as our horse seems to, because we can look directly at the ground beneath us. Though, our horses can spot something out on the distant horizon that we did not notice until we felt our horse tense up and look in that direction with his ears pricked.

This large view around them allows them to see us riding them. They can see as well as feel what our legs, hands, whip and even body are doing... even more so when they are bending on a circle.

Because they cannot see directly under their nose, some horses will get startled if you reach for their nose, or any place on their face coming from down there. This is also why they are given whiskers... so they know when their nose is close to something.

The horses' eyes can work separately, each taking in its own scene. Human eyes can only see one thing at a time, working together.

Horses' eyes are designed to pick up details of movement. This is of course, to protect themselves from predators hiding in a bush, in the deep grass or behind a rock. Movements unfamiliar to a horse will always cause reactions. The intensity of the reaction will depend on the horse's personality, age, maturity level and training.

The horse has to move his head around a lot in order to get things in clear focus. Horses focus the best through the upper part of their eyes, where the light is best positioned to help them see the definition of objects. This is why to focus on something far away, a horse will lift their heads up . Conversely, to see a treat being offered them, they will lower or arch their necks and tip their noses in so they can use the topmost part of their eyes.

Knowing this about horses, we can see how young ones panic if they are put in "bitting rigs" which require them to keep their heads still. Horses can learn, without restraint, to keep their heads in a general space. They learn to use other senses to guard themselves from predators, and they learn to trust their trainer in time.

Young horses are always more prone to be uptight and flighty with unfamiliar surroundings. Older horses who are used to the whole "scene" will be far harder to spook.

The horses' pupils are not round like ours. They are in a horizontal slit. This is to be able to shrink glaring light without reducing what he can see. If you have looked into the horse's eyes when you are outside, you will notice "blobs" floating in the eye. That is called the corpora nigra and they act like sunglasses to the horse.

Horses are not color blind. They can see yellows and greens the best, reds and blues the second best and are not very good at seeing purples, but still do. They do not particularly respond to different colors, but do react to extreme light and dark objects. A glaring white gate or white plastic bag will be far more spooky than say a brown paper bag.

Horses can see very well in the dark. Good night vision is a must for a prey animal. They can see well due to their large eyes and a special light-intensifying devise that reflects light back onto the retina... making the most of what is available.

However, horses to not adapt as quickly as we do to sudden changes of dark and light. This should always be remembered so we do not ever ask to much of our horse in situations where they will have to face this predicament.

Smell & Taste

A horse cannot breathe through his mouth, only through his nose, so their faces are built long which leaves a lot of room for the nasal cavities. This unique anatomy gives the horse sensitivity to smell that is likely to amaze us. The horse is also equipped with very large nostrils that can expand to capture as much scent and possible.

Scent is a very significant to they way a horse processes information, whether it be communication and recognition of herd members and scents of approaching predators, or the scent of water in the distance.

Horses like familiar scents. A horse loves a stable and a pasture that smells like their herd. The smell of manure can also signal to a wild horse what territory is his own herds', and which is not.

Smell and taste work together to be sure the horse is always eating things that are healthy and not harmful to him. This is why some horses refuse to eat their grain if a new powder or supplement is put into it.

The world of the horse is much like the dog's... scent being a very important part of life. For example, odors help a mare and a foal recognize each other. At birth, the foal is imprinted with licking and nuzzling by his mother, so she can memorize the foals scent and be able to recognize him from the other foals, even at night.

Rolling is another common scent orientated habit of horses. When a horse rolls, he is covering himself in the scent of the herd, creating unity and familiararity in the group.

When horses sniff each others' noses, they can easily identify each other as a friend or a threat. When a new horse is put out in the pasture, or when your horse sees new horses at a show, you will notice that is the first thing they do to each other is sniff noses. It is a getting to know you technique!

Horses are fussy eaters because of their sense of taste. It is much the same as ours, with taste buds on our tongues, palate and throat. They taste four flavors: salt, bitter, sweet and sour. Mixed with impressions of smell and texture, a complete assessment of the substance is built. Horses like sweet and salty, but so not like sour and bitterness. Most poisonous plants have a sour, bitter taste which is why most times they will not consume them.

This "pickiness" horses have is a life-saving devise because if a horse were to eat something that doesn't settle well, colic or blood poisoning could occur, because the horse cannot vomit.

The horse's sensitivity to smell and taste are incredibly useful tools for the day to day task of staying safe, healthy and happy!

Section 2

Beginning a Partnership
Handling Horses

Student Grace and her horse Gunner George

Hitting it Off

Starlin Afire (Afire Bey V x Sweet Promises) with Student, Maddie and her mom Lynn.
Photo by Leslie Hodgson.

The way you handle a horse (halter, catch, lead, tie, and groom) is very important. It begins your communication to the horse and lets them know what kind of person you are.

Even before we get on a horse's back, we can begin to create a harmonious partnership. Our attitude around the horse affects how he perceives us—and we want him to perceive us as respectable, dignified and loving. The horse can expect that if we are kind and considerate to them 'on the ground', that we will be that way when we ride.

That being said, we should apply the "golden rule" when we are around and riding horses. 'Do unto others as you would have them do unto you'. What we desire from the horse is cooperation and contribution. So, going along with the golden rule, let us give cooperation and contribution to the horse.

In all your time around horses, seek to serve their wants

and needs. Humans can tend to be a little "bossy" and sometimes we want something for nothing. This attitude will not work
if we want a horse to "partner up" with us. We must be unself-
ish—always putting their needs before our own.

We must cooperate with their nature and instincts. To do
that, we must understand them and respect their nature and instincts by not ever doing anything that is contrary to their nature.

We must contribute to the relationship with the horse by
being respectful to, and caring of them. This will make it possible
for them to be respectful to us.

The next "how-to's" are easy and fun to learn. All of these
things are done the way they are to be in accordance with the
horse's nature and instincts. We want the horses to be happy and
comfortable, right? Learn these well and always remember the
golden rule.

Catching

Whether we are catching the horse in a stall or a pasture,
they need to be approached with careful consideration. Remember, we are potential predators and they are a prey animal. To not
startle the horse, it is important to know where a horse can and
can't see us:

DIAGRAM OF THE HORSE'S BLIND SPOTS

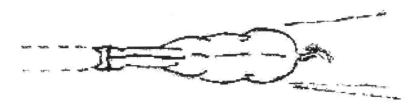

Definitely a wrong place to approach the horse is directly

45

behind him. In the pasture, there will be enough room for you to be able to walk around the horse so you are in his line of vision. In the stall, if the horse is facing away from you, get his attention by talking to him and encourage him to turn around.

The safest place to approach a horse is walking towards his shoulder.

When we are going to catch a horse, we must be aware of our own body language. Horses talk to each other through body language. (See Section 1) We too can talk to the horse through body language.

Being aware of the horses sensitivity to our body language, we must be cautious of how we talk to them. When we jump up and down and flail our arms around, it would be the same as a horse bucking, rearing and striking to keep other horses away from them. Also, we can make them move away from us by look-ing them square in the eye, squaring up our shoulders, crouching a little lower and moving towards them head and shoulders lead-ing.

So, naturally, when we want to catch the horse, we should look as inviting and approachable as we can. Once you get next to the horse, use a kind voice so he keeps being reminded you are his friend and you are not going to hurt him. Then, it is a good idea to slip the rope calmly over his neck. This will help you secure him if he decides to walk away or something startles him until you get the halter on.

Despite your good efforts, still some horses might shy away. Be patient. Be calm. Assure the horse that he should not be afraid of you in any way. Seek help from another person if the horse is being really impossible to catch, all the while remembering to be the dignified leader so the horse will trust and respect you.

Haltering

1) Stand on the left side & put the rope around his neck

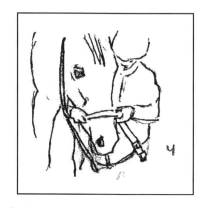

2) Place the horse's nose in the round part of the halter

3) Slide hands up to the top buckles and "fling" the strap over his ears.

4) Use both hands to put the buckle through

5) How tight? Two fingers below the cheek bone

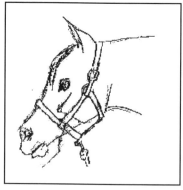

6) Secure the strap and you are ready for take-off!

Leading

Be the Leader

Remember, horses are a herd animal. They stay together in groups and they get led by a leader of the herd. The horses in the herd will submit to whoever has the strongest personality and to the one who "takes charge" (most often the "Lead Mare").

Horses need and want that trait in us. They need a leader. They want a leader. If we know how to communicate to the horse properly and "speak his language" to get him to do what we desire, the horse will gladly follow and obey.

Look at all the amazing examples we have of this being true. Have you ever watched Dressage at the Olympics? Or how about those horses going over those huge jumps? Have you ever seen a show like Cavalia™? Or, have you ever seen a big horse being led around by a small little child? Have you ever marveled at how brave and well trained war horses are? Have you ever been amazed that horses are so well behaved and have worked so hard for our transportation throughout the ages?

These are all evidence of how willing and trainable horses are. Again, when you learn how to communicate and how to become a great leader, you and your horse can become a successful team.

We must be:
- Patient & Quiet
- Clear and Concise
- Impassive and Strong
- Attentive and Alert
- Assertive not Aggressive

How to hold the rope

Proper "Figure 8" Loops

Improper Circular Loops

Hold the rope with your right hand right below the snap. This is how you are going to guide the horse. Hold the excessrope in "figure eight" loops. If you hold the excess in circular loops around your hand, and the horse pulls away, the rope will tighten around your hand and maybe cause damage. The figure eight loops allow the rope to slip through your hands.

Backing the Horse Up

1) Turn around and face the back of the horse.

2) Switch the rope in your hands (Left hand below snap, right hand on excess rope).

3) Place your right hand on the horse's point of shoulder.

4) Begin gently pulling at the halter by the rope towards his chest. At the same time, nudge his shoulder with your right hand and say "back" or cluck.

Turning the Horse

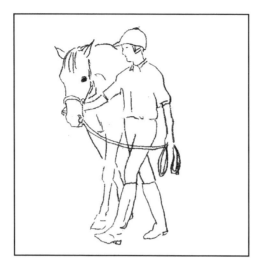

To turn the horse towards you, simply turn and they should follow. Make sure that the horse does not crowd you, or you will be in danger of getting your feet stepped on. Keep your eyes up!

To turn the horse away from you, straighten out your arm and "walk into his face". Nudge on the halter if you have to, to get the horse to turn away from the pressure. Ask the horse stay slow and turning on his hindquarters so you can easily stay in front of him and in control.

Controlling the Horse

Some horses can have a hard time standing still for very long and some horses can spook easily. These following tips will help you stay safe and in control.

"Personal Bubble"

Horses are big animals! Sometimes, for different reasons they might try to get a little too close to you. Some just love to "snuggle" and want to rub on you, nibble on you and just get petted. This is cute, yes, but sometimes they might catch you unaware and knock you to the ground, bonk your head, push you against a wall or fence, and sometimes the nibbling turns to biting. It's great that the horse can think of us as such a friend, but we need to remind them that we are not horses!

Do not let the horse rub on you, or get right up next to your feet and face or to nibble on you. There are plenty of other ways for them to show and receive affection. Keep him out of your "personal bubble" with clarity of what you want and persistence and consistency. The horse will still be able to get rubbed and kissed and loved on, but you need to initiate it, and try to rub and scratch them on their neck, shoulders, and body. That way you are out of the line of fire from their head and teeth that they use on other horses to show love, trust, and affection.

Another invasion of your personal bubble that can happen is when the horse gets spooked. They will crowd you either because they "forget you are there" in a way, or they look to you for protection the same way a foal always runs back to his mother when he is scared of something or has felt threatened.

We are too small and light to "push" the horse back out of our bubble, so we must use horse language to get them to move out. Throw up your hands and square your shoulders with them to keep them away. After they are back in their OWN personal bubble, you can reward him with a "Good Boy" and continue on. You can use your voice to assure him he can still trust you and you will have earned his respect by not letting him trample you.

Remember when the horse spooks, don't let yourself get spooked. Stay calm. Stay emotionally detached and nonchalant and the horse will begin to calm and mimic your attitude after a while.

A common problem that small handlers have when trying to keep a horse standing still, is letting the horse walk around them in circles, invading their personal bubble.

To avoid this happening, keep the horse's head straight in front of him. Many find it easier to face the horse like you are going to back him up. Each time the horse does try to walk forward, put his head straight in front of his shoulders and body and then back him up a step or two. Then always remember to reward him when he has settled, even for a short time into the place you want him to be.

Tying

The Quick Release Knot

This is always the knot we use to tie up the horse. We use it because if the horse starts to panic, we can release them hopefully before they hurt themselves and/or the objects they are tied to.

1) Put rope in or around object & make loop

2) Put loop around and through & PULL TIGHT

3) More loops if prefered.

4) Pull rope to release.

Tying Safety
The Right Height

If a horse is tied too low, he can reach the ground to graze, and then he might step over or on his rope. Again, a horse does not like to be trapped... and he will feel his head being stuck by the rope and begin to panic. Injury to the horse can occur.

The Right Length
That also being said, it is important to make sure the rope is tied at the proper length. You don't want your horse to be able to move around a lot. They should be able to move their head, but not walk back and forth along the fence or wall. A risk of the rope being too long is again, that the horse will get his leg over it and get stuck. It might be wise to not let your horse graze when he is tied up to avoid him getting his leg over, or stepping on the rope.

A risk of the rope being too tight is that if the horse can't move his head and see what is going on around him, he will start to panic and pull back on the rope, then that added pressure increases their panicking.

The Right Area
A horse should never be tied where they can injure themselves on sharp objects or get their legs caught in anything. Tie your horse in a safe, clean area.

A horse tied at the right height and the right length.

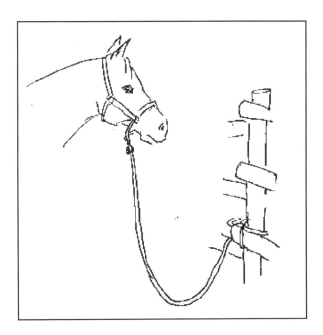

A horse tied too low and too long. This is very unsafe and can cause the horse harm.

Grooming

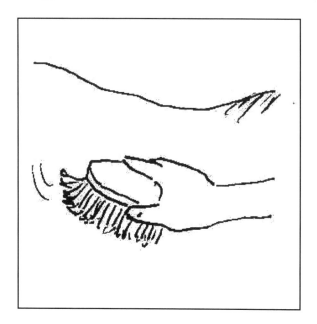

Grooming is good for stimulating the muscles and the coat of the horse. Groom before you ride to remove mud or dirt from the saddle and girth area, so your horse does not get sores.

Grooming is a great time to thoroughly inspect your horse, so you know that he is in good health. Also, grooming is yet another way to communicate to your horse your love and intentions. It can be a wonderful bonding time.

Grooming Tools
Tool #1 = **Curry Comb**

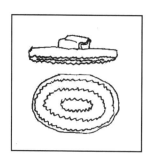

Purposes of the Curry Comb:
- To loosen the dirt from the skin and hair so that it can more easily be brushed away.
- To massage the muscles and the coat to stimulate circulation so that the horses coat will grow more healthy and shine!

How to use the Curry Comb:

A curry comb is used in circular motions. This is how to best loosen the dirt and hair because it will "capture" all that you curry over. If you just go back and forth, the dirt will instead get rubbed in.

On the horse, you can use the curry comb anywhere there is a lot of muscle tone like the neck, the sides, and the hindquarters. It might be uncomfortable for the horse for you to use them over their lower legs or their face where it would go straight to the bone. If you were cautious and needed to use the curry in those areas to say get off caked mud, then exceptions could be made. Though, in regular grooming, it is not necessary to curry the horse's lower legs or their face.

The different kinds of curry combs:

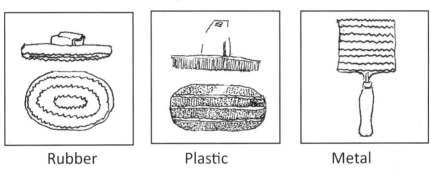

| Rubber | Plastic | Metal |

Metal Curry Comb: This curry comb is used differently than the rubber curry combs because it has metal "teeth". You might notice that in the winter when the horse's coat is long that it is really hard to curry off caked mud and dirt because it seems to just cling to the hair or just turn into huge mounds of dust and dirt... this is when the metal curry comb is heavenly to have. You just do long strokes and fling that dirt and hair right off. It will gently loosen the mud from the hair and push it off your horse to the ground.

Tool #2—**Hard Brush**

Purposes of the Hard Brush
• To sweep away the dirt and hair brought up off the skin by the curry comb.

How to use the Hard Brush:

Use short, "flinging" motions starting at the poll, and going to the tail, covering all areas in between. Use your writst to "fling" the brush. If you didn't fling, the dirt would just stay on your horse! Depending on just how hard those bristles are, you should again not use the hard brush on the face or below the knee.

Tool #3—Soft Brush

Purposes of the Soft Brush
• To brush the areas that the curry comb and hard brush could not get: below the knee and the horses face.
• To "polish" the coat.

How to use the Soft Brush:

Gently brush over the lower legs and face using only a small fling, so that you can stay close to the horse and not get sloppy and accidentally bonk him in the eye or in the cannon bone.

Go over the whole horse again starting at the poll to gently brush away any loose dirt or hairs that the hard bristles of the hard brush missed. This will make your horse gleam!

Tool #4—**Mane and Tail Brush**

Purposes of the Mane and Tail Brush:
• To get the knots and tangles out of the horse's mane, tail and forelock.

How to use the Mane and Tail Brush:

Horses' hair has thicker strands than human hair, and they have fewer nerve endings in the areas that the hair grows from... so, we can use a little more force than we do with our own sensitive scalps.

When you start at the top, you can get a huge knot in the mane or tail by the time you get to the bottom (if you even can). In that case:
• Start at the ends of the hair and work your way up.
• Do the bottom section until it is smooth and then move up about 8-9 inches and brush that out until that is smooth.
• TIP: Its much easier to get the tangles out if you have a detangler spray.

Tool #5—**Hoof Pick**

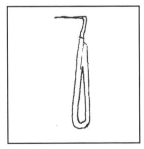

Purposes of the Hoof Pick:
• To get dirt, mud, rocks or anything that can get in the horse's hoof out.

How to pick up the horses hoof:

1) Stand facing the back of the horse Place your hand on his shoulder or hindquarters and begin to run your hand down his leg. You don't want to reach out and GRAB the horse's leg. They are a prey animal and predators can bring them down and wound them by grabbing onto their legs. So don't act like a predator to your horse by just reaching out and grabbing his leg. If you start at the shoulder or hindquarters, he will know you are coming and you will not frighten him.

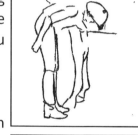

2) Some horses will pick up their legs that easily. Others need a little incentive, so: lean on the horses shoulder so that he shifts his weight to the other hoof, then "squeeze" either his tendons in the back of his leg below his knee, or pinch the chestnut on the inside of the leg.

3) Front Leg: When the horse starts to lift his hoof up, slide your hand down and aid him in pulling his hoof off the ground.

4) Hold and support the horse's hoof at the coronary band and begin cleaning. (See cleaning the hoof on the following page.)

Hind Leg: When the horse lifts his hoof up, move your leg in to help support the leg so you can pick the hoof.

How to "pick" or clean-out the horses hoof:

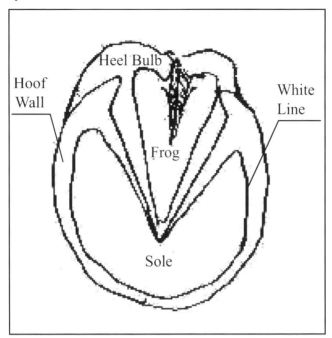

DIAGRAM OF THE HORSE'S HOOF

Wall: The wall of the horse's hoof is strong. This is why they can handle tough terrain and is how it is possible for them to get metal shoes put on with nails. The horse does not feel those nails at all. Try squeezing the tip of your fingernail just by itself, pinch it or do whatever... your finger knows you are there, but your actual finger nail can feel nothing. So, we don't need to worry about the wall so much when we are picking the horse's hoof, especially since there is usually a shoe there.

Sole: The sole however, is sensitive. The wall of the hoof is what hits the ground, so it protects the sole from hitting the ground. Shoes help get the sole more off the ground. When a horse's sole steps on a rock, you will see them be tender on it at that moment. Sometimes the sole can get bruised, but if the horse has a strong hoof wall and/or shoes, that can be avoided.

Frog: The frog is another sensitive part of the hoof. Unlike the hoof wall and sole, the frog is somewhat "squishy". It is in a triangular shape starting at the heel bulbs and pointing down.

1) Start at the top and point the hoof pick away from you

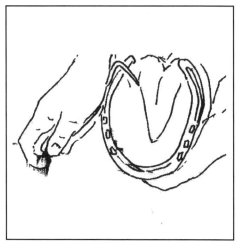

2) Use strong downward motions in a triangle around the frog

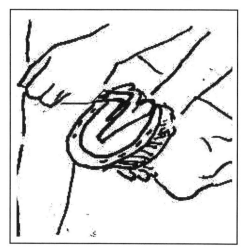

A horse's hooves should always be inspected and cleaned if they live in a rocky area, or if they are in their stalls a lot. Rocks can cause bruises, and wetness from the stalls can cause thrush and abcesses.

Inspecting Your Horse

A great time to inspect your horse is when you are grooming. To do this, we use two of our own tools: our eyes and our hands.

It is easy to see if a horse has a gash or a cut, a burn or a sore. It is a little more difficult to see swelling because it is not as obvious. We can also watch how the horse moves with our eyes. Learn to know your horse when he is feeling great and how he moves, so that you can catch sicknesses early or see that he is wounded and get treatment for him right away. We need to be aware of all of these things with our eyes.

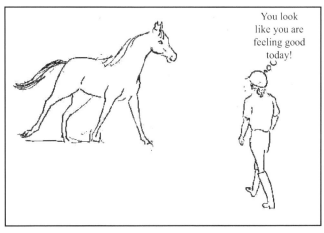

With our hands, while we are grooming, we touch the horse and feel for any heat or swelling. If you think you do feel the heat or swelling, compare it by touching the same part on the other side of the horse's body. For example, if you feel heat or swelling in the right fore fetlock, then compare it by touching the left fore fetlock, and you can even check the hind ones as well. Usually, if all four are the same temperature, there is probably nothing wrong with the horse, unless you see him walking tenderly or acting strangely.

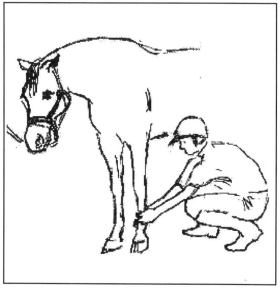

Report any suspicious signs or obvious wounds to your instructor, or any person that can get attention for the horse. Refer to the upper level manuals for first aid treatment.

Grooming Safety Rules

• **Never get down on your knees or sit down around the horse's feet.** If the horse spooks at something and you are on your knees or sitting down, it is really hard to get up fast and out of the way. So, to keep from getting stepped on, stay on your feet and just bend over if you need to get low. That way, if the horse spooks big enough that you need to get out of the way, you can do it quickly.

• **Let the horse know where you are at all times.** Remember, the horse is a prey animal and is always cautious of the things around him. Don't startle him by reaching out and touching him when he can't see you or he doesn't know where you are.

The ways you can let him know where you are is with your voice and your touch. If you are going to cross into his blind spots, keep a hand on him and/or talk to him so he doesn't lose track of you.

• **Don't stand directly behind the horse to brush his tail.** Bring his tail around to the side.

• **"Over".** If your horse's body is too close to a wall or to a fence, you shouldn't squeeze in there because the horse can squish you very easily. So, we can ask the horse to "move over".

Gently put one hand on the side of his shoulder, and one hand on his barrel, and nudge him and say "over". Most horses listen to this light urging. But, if your horse doesn't, then nudge a little harder and lean a little on him if you have to. Remember... be the leader!

Section 3
Harmony in Riding

"Let the love for the feeling of responsibility toward the horse rule all your decisions and actions." –Egon von Neindorff

"Our riding will always radiate beauty and joyfulness when we are motivated by respect and love for the horse."
–Erik Herbermann, Dressage Formula

Riding is about...

Riding can be a very beautiful thing. Horse and rider unite, radiant with happiness and kindness. When done correctly with true passion and dedication, it turns into an art.

Riding is about overcoming barriers within yourself to reach what you desire—complete oneness with the horse. It might only come in glimpses at first, but then you can take those glimpses and have them last into moments. Then, one day, you might have the best ride you have ever had.

You will experience the definition of "the best ride" when you and the horse feel completely independent, though completely "together" all at the same time. You are thinking the same things, reading each other's minds. You are setting and attaining your goals together.

Riding a horse gives us such marvelous opportunities to reach inside ourselves and become the best person we can be.

Riding Requires:
- Patience
- Determination
- Passion
- Talent
- Dedication
- Self-Control
- Willingness
- Time

SRF Make Myne Mynk galloping with Leslie

Riding is all about feeling. Horses and humans are not built alike. In fact, we are very different physically and mentally. Riding is attempting to take these very different beings of horse and human and unite them.

This makes our task as the rider very important and not to

70

be taken lightly. If we truly are motivated by respect for and love of the horse then we can and WILL take on the task of becoming a great rider.

Riding, when done correctly, with clear purpose in mind can enhance the horse's well-being and beauty. What better motive can we have than that? Just think... it is possible for us to take a creature already majestic and beautiful by nature and develop it... making it even more beautiful than it was before. This is how we become artists.

This can only be done through study, application and practice of correct theories and methods. If you really love horses and riding and practice to attain ALL the character traits listed above, you will have much joy and success along your path. Technique gives you a path to let your emotions and dedication show. Master technique so you can show the world what you love.

Besides having to learn physical and technical applications to ride well—perhaps the most important lessons you will learn are the mental applications. Riding correctly is a way of thinking.

As humans we have an undesirable quality where we put blocks in between our physical and our mental aspects. Gratefully, horsemanship can help us become balanced between mind, body and spirit. To achieve this of course, we must be dedicated, diligent and willing.

We must open our minds—relax and listen to the language of the horse and our own bodies. Our minds should be guided by this language so we can always be seeking for these glimpses of true harmony.

Preparing to Ride -Tacking Up
Saddling

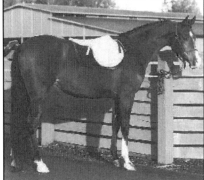

1) Saddle Pads On
There are many different shapes of pads for many different shapes of saddles. You always want saddle pads on your horse to prevent soreness and chaffing. Make sure they are not too far back, or too far forward. This picture shows where the saddle pads should sit. Keep your saddle pads clean and dry.

2) Saddle On
Set your saddle gently onto the horse. Do not slam it on. This would instantly start your ride off in the wrong way. You want your horse to know you are considerate of his comfort. Place the saddle in the correct place. It should rest nicely behind your horse's shoulder blades and not pinch him anywhere.

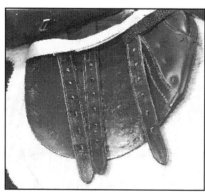

3) Secure Straps
Most saddle pads have nylon straps on them to secure on the saddle. Velcroe around the sweat flap or around the first billet, or slide the first billet through the nylon strap. Securing these straps will assure that the pads don't slip out from underneath the saddle.

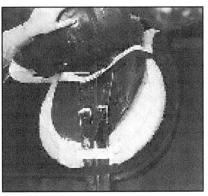

4) Girth on the RIGHT SIDE. You start by putting the girth on the right side of the horse, with the NON-ELASTIC side. You want to be able to tighten the other side. If the saddle has loops on the bottom, slide the girth up through them. What hole? The buckles on the elastic side should hang down and touch the bottom of the horses fetlock. Use the first and third billets.

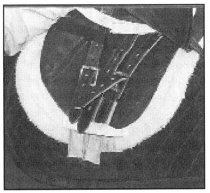

5) Cinch Up. Walk around to the other side of your horse and reach under to grab the girth. Put it through the loops if your pads have them, then use the first buckle to put on the first billet, and the second buckle put on the third billet. It is curteous to the horse not to tighten it up too much at first. It should only be tight enough to keep the saddle on until you get to the riding area to tighten it.

6) Overview. Make sure everything is secured and in the right place. The girth should be right behind your horse's elbows. The pads should be straight and smooth. Fix anything that needs to be fixed.

73

Bridling

1) Put the Halter Around the Neck. Unbuckle the halter, let it drop off the horse's nose, then rebuckle it around their neck. This is to keep the horse from moving or running off. If you are in the cross-ties, unfasten the crosstie on the left side which you will be standing on.

2) Prepare to Put the Bit In. Hold the reins in your arm, or put them over the horses's head. You can either wrap your right hand around the horse's head as shown in this picture and then hold the bridle by the cheekpieces, or you can hold the crownpeice with your right hand between the horse's ears. Use your right hand and arm to keep the horse's head steady if they try to move around.

3) Put the Bit In. Use your left hand and open up the bit and hold it flat. Make sure the bit is in the crack of the horse's teeth so when they open their mouths, the bit can slide in and you won't hurt their gums. If the horse will not open his mouth, slide your thumb in and push on the horse's tongue. Don't worry, the horses does not have teeth right there. They only have the front incisors and the back molars.

4) Put the Crownpeice Over Ears. After the bit has gone into the horses mouth, gently draw the bridle up and use your hands to put their ears in the bridle. The bit should rest so that there is exactly one or two small wrinkles in the corners of their mouth. Use the cheekpieces to make adjustments if necessary. Make sure the bit is even and that the browband or any part of the bridle is not pinching or poking.

5) Buckle Up Caveson.
The noseband needs to be two finger's measurements from the cheekbone. Then cinch up the caveson snug but not too tight. A standard measurement for tightness is that you can fit two fingers in between the horse's jawline and the caveson nice and snuggly. You want to be able to get your two fingers in... but only two, not three or four!

6) Buckle Up Throatlatch.
The throat latch is used to keep the bridle from coming over the ears and falling off. It needs to be snug enough to do its job, but shouldn't be tight. Standard measurement is one fist in between the throat and the throat latch. Again, only *one* fist that touches the leather and the horse's throat comfortably.

Beginning Your Ride the Right Way
Mounting the Horse

Before we mount, there are three important things to do. While you do these first three steps, keep holding the reins in your hand so your horse does not step on them or get away.

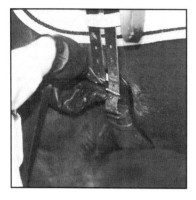

1. Tighten Girth: If you are not tall enough or strong enough to do this by yourself, remember to ask your instructor to tighten it for you. It is your responsibility to make sure this gets done. Watch what your instructor does so that when you are strong and tall enough, you can do it by yourself.

2. Pull stirrups down and check length. A good hunter length is to put your knuckles up at buckles of the stirrup leathers and straighten out your arm. If the stirrup hits your armpit when you pull it out, it is a good length. Dressage, a little longer... jumping, a little shorter. You can always adjust them when you get on as well.

3. Put the reins over your horse's head. Remember that your horse's ears are "floppy" and if you are not tall enough, you can pull the reins over their ears. Be considerate of your horse and do this smoothly and quickly. Some horses don't like their ears to be touched so, keep that in mind as well.

Mounting

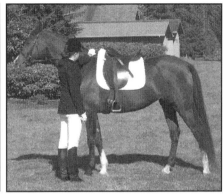

Stand on left side of the horse. It is a rule that we always mount and dismount from the left side of our horse.

Gather reins in left hand and take a hold of the mane with the same hand.

3) Put left foot in stirrup and lift self up gently

4) Land gently in the saddle.

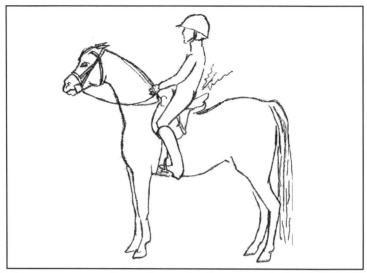

We do not want to be rude to the horse by just slamming down on his back. Remember, we want happy horses that want to work for and with us. If we just slam down on his back right when we get on, then we have already started off our exercise in contention with the horse.

If we land gently we are letting the horse know that we care about them and want to keep a good partnership.

Picking Up and Shortening Your Reins

Picking Up Your Reins

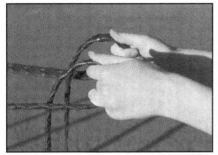 

Correct "Thumbs Up"   Incorrect (Upside Down)

Shortening Your Reins

Take your right fingers and hold the left rein **behind** the left hand.

Then **slide** your left hand up the rein and re-grip the rein sturdily.

Now, do the same to the right rein; Use your left fingers to hold the right rein **behind** your right hand.

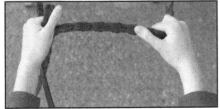

Then **slide** your hand up the rein to "shorten it".

Do not "crawl" up the reins. When you do this, you are opening your fingers up for too long. The horse can pull the reins very quickly out of your hands if he trips or spooks or just wants to pull down. Then you wouldn't have control. By doing it how the first example showed us, we keep a firm grip on the reins at all times.

Picking Up Your Stirrups

Pick up stirrups WITHOUT using your hands. Place the stirrups on the balls of your feet, again without using hands.

Lift your foot up into the arch of the stirrup. Bring the stirrup away from your horse using your foot on the outside of the iron. Then press down onto the stirrup pad to secure your "catch".

Stirrups on Arch (Incorrect)   Stirrups on Ball of Foot (Correct)

Dismounting

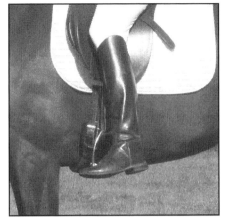

1) Take both feet out of stirrups.

2) Hold reins in left hand.

3) Swing down to the left side.

4) Roll up stirrups.

5) Loosen girth.

6) Loosen caveson.

Your Form:
The Ultimate Influence
on the Horse

If you truly love and care for the horse, you will take having good form and acquiring a good seat very seriously, or you can hinder instead of enhance the horse. Horses have wonderful, beautiful motion. Watching them run free is a captivating experience. That can all change when a human sits on their back, unless we learn where and how to sit and aid.

It is our task as the more intelligent of the partnership to move beyond ourselves and become as completely "horse-like" as possible. Because of our intelligence, we can understand how the horse's body works and then take upon us to unite us. We

can only encourage and invite this harmony. When force starts...
beauty ends.

Let us now learn about each of our anatomy's and how to
unite together. If you look at the way we are built and the way a
horse is built... to say the least, it is very different!!!

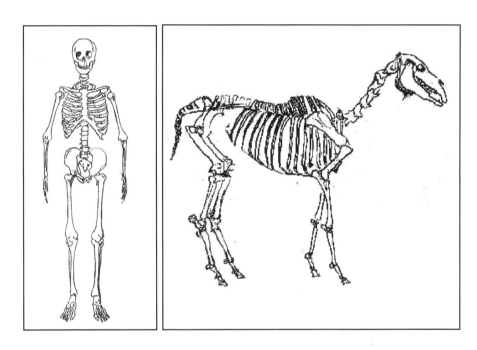

Horses walk on four legs and their spines are parallel to the
ground. Humans walk on two legs and our spines are perpendicu-
lar to the ground.

Riding is attempting to connect these two very different
creatures and unite them in perfect "harmony".

Your Seat

Our seat is the connecting point between us and the horse. When we ride, we should think of our bodies as the control center. It is not our job to force the horse and to push or shove him to do what we ask him to. If we take our body as it is now and just stick it on top of the horse... that would be exactly what we would do. We would be stiff, rough, un-giving, and in short, make the horse uncomfortable when they carry us.

We must connect ourselves to the horse in a way that they are comfortable, and in a way that we can have the most influence on their gait, speed, stride and direction.

We must attempt to become ONE with our horse. What does that mean? We must CONNECT our self to the horse. This is done through the seat.

Your seat is a reflection of your mental and emotional attitudes, if you are tense in mind, you will be tense in body. If you are upset or angry, your form will be jagged and rigged. Your mental self and your physical self are inseparable.

First Step:

You must LET your weight REST into the DEEPEST part of your saddle. Take your feet out of the stirrups and let your legs hang straight down. It is common for humans to want to carry our weight all in our upper body when we are on a horse.

However, we must put our weight where it will help us and the horse stay balanced.

Sitting in the Horse's Center of Gravity

Weight

It is not only more comfortable for your weight to be in the lower part of your body, but it is also safer. Imagine your weight as sand, which makes you pretty heavy. If you keep all that weight in your upper body and your horse spooks and jumps to the side, you will tip right over.

Now, let all that sand sift down evenly to each of your legs and your seat. Now what happens if your horse spooks? You are anchored around your horse and you don't budge when the horse jumps to the side!

It's just like a punching bag! All the sand is down at the bottom. When you punch the top of the bag, the top can move, but the bag stays where it is because it is heavy, almost like it is anchored to the ground.

So, you must anchor yourself to the horse by putting your weight where it is the most comfortable and safe for both you and the horse. **Stretch UP, Weight DOWN.**

This illustration depicts the weight of this rider being carried in the upper body. Doesn't that look unstable? Riding like this will cause you to be unbalanced and prone to falling off.

This illustration depicts the weight of this rider being carried in the lower body. This definitely looks stable. Keeping your weight DOWN will anchor you to the horse. You will stay with its every movement because you are balanced and comfortable.

The triangle is made up of three bones in your seat. Two seat bones, and the front bone. Your weight should be **evenly distrubuted** on these bones.

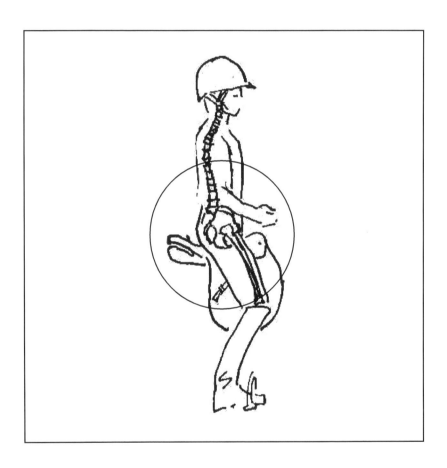

If they are not even, you will not be straight or balanced in the horse's center of gravity. The following are common mistakes of riders. Look at how they affect our position and seat.

Fork Seat ("Duck Butt")

Rounded Back ("Chair Seat")

Correct and Balanced Triangle

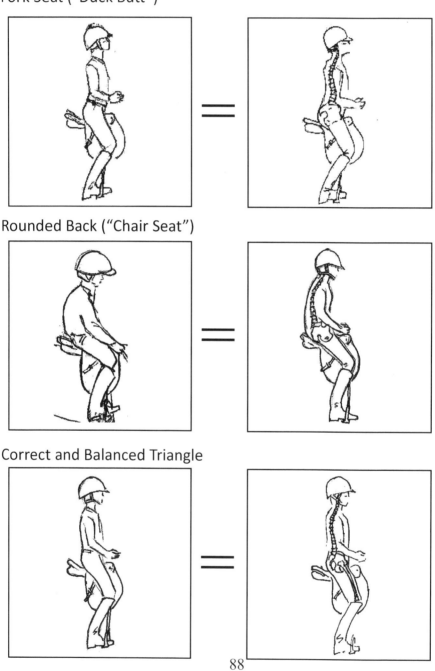

Our Hips

Our hips are a fantastic joint. They are just like our shoulder. They rotate and can actually get popped out (not one of the most comfortable things). We need to understand this about our hips, so that we do not think they are just stuck and unmovable when we ride. They, along with our knees and ankles make it possible for us to walk, run, jump, skip and most importantly, RIDE, right?!

In all the great Dressage Books, they always suggest that you imagine turning your hips into something else. "Mobile flippers" (*Centered Riding*), "Water" (*Dressage Formula*). Whatever you decide to turn them into in your mind should be something that MOVES.

Another good one is "Shock Absorbers". Most kids don't really know what shock absorbers are in a car. We'll tell and show you. Shock absorbers make it possible for the wheels to move up and down going over bumps so that the car can stay pretty much going flat. The wheels do all the bumping up and down while the car stays relatively smooth.

If we are to weld ourselves to the horse (the saddle), we cannot do it stiffly. It just doesn't work. If we are stiff on the horse, we become a pogo stick. It's fun and comfortable at the trot if you are like jello and just "boogie" with the motion, but if you tense up you start bouncing very uncomfortably, then it is a little more difficult to stay on!

We must let our hips become SHOCK ABSORBERS. They must MOVE. They will allow the horse to move freely and beautifully if we can let our hips do the same thing.

Do you think we should force them to move? No. We should LET them move by RELAXING them. The best time to practice this is on a lunge line with the help of an instructor. Just turn your hips to water and let them move. **Stay close to the horse.**

Putting Your Seat and Hips Together

A perfectly correct seat takes years to acquire, and even then, it takes constant practice to maintain. It is ok if you have a day that is "off". You must not get frustrated when the work gets hard. Every day when you ride, attempt to acquire a better seat. You cannot ever attain it if you don't give it your best everyday.

"Practice does not make perfect.
PERFECT PRACTICE MAKES PERFECT."
Wade B. Cook

Let's remember now: Your triangle is "stuck" to the saddle. At the walk, sitting trot, and canter, we should never be able to see "air" between the saddle and your seat. At the rising (posting) trot, you should stay close to the saddle so you can stay relatively close to the horse at all times. To acheive this, don't post very high and stay relaxed yet poised.

Your hips are the shock absorbers that let the motion of the horse travel through us so your seat can stay in the saddle at the sitting trot, walk and canter, and close to the saddle at the rising trot.

Sit Evenly
• To be balanced
• To stay on the horse
• To make it easier for the horse to travel straight. You want the horse to travel straight so they can build up the correct muscles. Imagine if you walked around with your left shoulder dropped and your ribs pushed out to the right and your head cocked to the right ALL THE TIME. If you did that for long enough, your muscles would get used to carrying you that way and it would be hard to do anything normally. It is the same with horses. It is your goal to have your horse always progress-ing and getting better through his gymnastic work. If you let him or cause him to travel around crookedly, he will never build up the correct muscles.
• To help YOU build up the correct muscles.

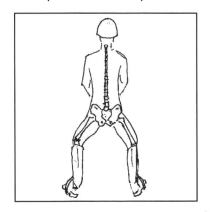 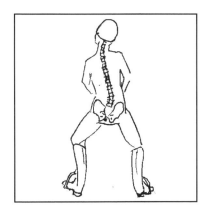

How:

Memorize and go through this checklist in your mind every time you ride to avoid burdening your horse and/or getting into bad riding habits.

Step 1—check that your stirrups are even and that you have EQUAL weight in both stirrups. Do not lean or step into one more than the other.

Step 2—Make sure that you have all your weight evenly distributed on your triangle.

Step 3—Have your hips straight and resting nicely upon even weighted seat bones.

Step 4—Keep your shoulders straight and open. Do not collapse either of your shoulders.

Step 5—Keep your head straight and eyes up… looking where you want to go at all times.

Step 6—Check our "Straight Lines"

"Straight Lines"

There are two straight lines that your form must show to know that you are sitting evenly and correctly in the saddle.

"Straight Line" #1:
"Ear, Shoulder, Hip, Seat Bones, Heel."

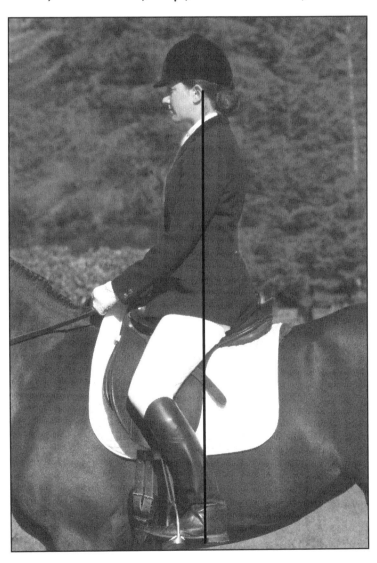

Common faults:

PUSHING into the stirrup

Not letting your ankle flex

Closed front line

Chin/Eyes Down

The basic answer to solve all of these issues is to keep your seat balanced correctly on the triangle, distribute your weight evenly and let it REST DOWN. Keep your 'front line' open... be dignified!

"Straight Line" #2:
Elbow, Hand, Bit

Your hand and elbow is to become part of the horse. To do that, you have to imagine the bit and rein becoming part of your arm, or your arms and fingers extending all the way to the bit.

 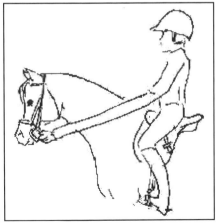

From our elbow to our knuckles should be one smooth

line. These "broken wrist" examples below are common faults that lead to many problems with the horse.

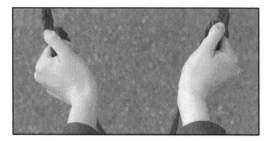

Broken/Twisted Out

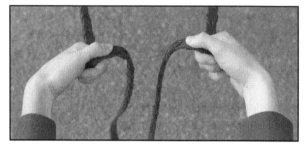

Rounded In

Piano Hands   Puppy Dog Hands

All of these broken wrist examples make it impossible to be one with the horse. Only when the wrists are relaxed and straight with our thumbs on top can we move with and become one with the horse. Holding our wrists wrong cause us to tense up muscles and twist our tendons and bones in a way that inhibits our motion.

If we can't move with the horse's movement, how can we expect to become one with him? Remember, we have to become as completely horse-like as possible. You want your hands and elbows to move with the horse's motion so you do not hinder him or make him feel trapped. It is still important to keep a nice contact with his mouth, but keep it inviting and encouraging with soft and supple hands.

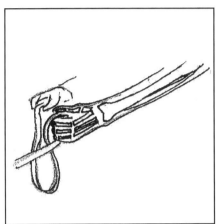 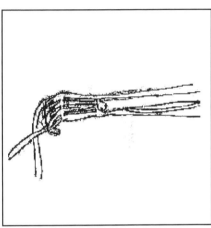

Keep Your Thumbs On Top

In the illustrations above, you can see the differences in the bones in your arm when you keep your "thumbs on top" and when your knuckles face up ("piano hands"). Thumbs on top creates no friction in your arm and gives you ease of motion back and forth. Knuckles on top causes bones and tendons in your arm to twist, which makes it difficult for movement back and forth to happen effortlessly.

Front Line

The front line starts under your chin and ends at your crotch. Remember these words when thinking of your front line: OPEN, STRETCHED, FREE and INDEPENDENT at all times. This cannot be stressed enough.

Too often we see riders crouched over their horse's withers. When we are not open, stretched, free and independent, we have become a burden for our horse to carry. Imagine instead having your upper body making a capital "D".

Open: Roll your shoulders back, open up your lungs. Your shoulders should be back and DOWN. Do not hold your shoulders up and tense. Give them to the horse and the motion.

Stretched: Don't collapse anywhere in your body. Keep every-thing straight and independent.

Free & Independent: Remember, all the weight is in your seat and legs, so this should LIBERATE your upper body to be able to move, turn (not collapse) around corners, t-point over fences, or anything you need it to do.

With our front line, we can encourage the horse to go for-ward. Think of it as arrows pointing out of it all the time, sending your horse exactly where he needs to go.

When your front line is collapsed, your horse's freedom of motion is disrupted. The horse will fall more on their forehand because that is where you are putting your weight. Also, sitting this way has put you out of the horse's center of gravity and they will have more of a job on their hands trying to balance you.

Having your front line open creates freedom for you and your horse. You will be lighter, balanced, and the horse will be pleased to carry you. The horse needs to stay "in front of your leg", and having an open front line can help accomplish this because you will be encourag-ing them to use their hindquarters more and be light and "up" with their shoulders.

Thigh and Knee

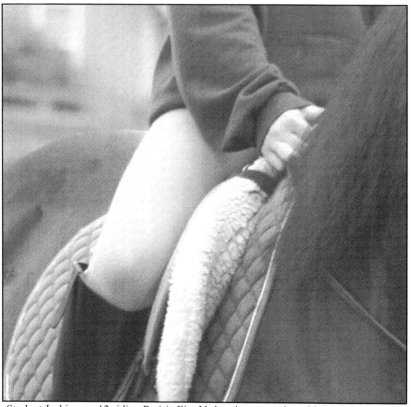

Student Jackie, age 12 riding Prairie Fire V showing exemplary thigh and knee position.

The most important thing to know about your thigh and knee position is that they cannot be correct unless you have a very relaxed hip joint. Your legs simply need to 'hang' down around the horse. Not sloppily of course. Remember, let your weight relax down to your seat and leg.

Getting the correct thigh feeling: Lift your leg up off the saddle, opening your hip joint wide, turn the lower leg inward (until your feet are parallel to the horse's side), and then lay your leg RELAXED again on the horse's side.

Knee Closed. Closed does not mean 'gripped' or 'clamped' it means nicely against the saddle so you cannot see air. Snuggle your knee gently into the saddle flap.

Opened Knee   Closed Knee

To keep the weight snuggled around your horse, imagine and direct the flowing energy from your hip out your knee, like when you are going down to kneel.

It is important to use your thigh and knee when you are riding. Again, do not "pinch" the horse with them, but keep them snug and put them to work. If you do this, you will not have to use your upper body, or your feet for the rising trot or the two-point, thereby creating an efforless and "quiet" look and feel to your riding.

Keep your knee bent in all the gaits. Do not lock it up and be stiff. Let it bend and be flexible, but stable.

Lower Leg and Foot

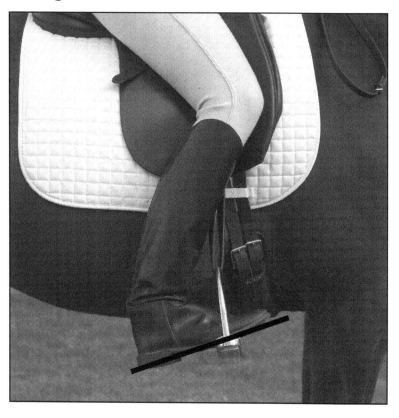

Place the stirrup on the ball of your foot. This is to give your foot leverage to be able to let your weight sink down into your heels. If you have the stirrup farther back, it is very difficult to bend your ankle. Having the stirrup anywhere other than the ball of your foot also throws off your "alignment".

"Heels down" is a very, very common thing you will hear a lot in your lessons. The heel should always be the lowest point of the rider. THIS SHOULD COME NATURALLY if you are sitting in your saddle correctly, with your "straight lines" and weight resting where it should.

You are to become a stretched, elastic person when you are riding horses. This is so that when the horse moves, you move with him and keep all these form corrections in place. This is especially applied to heels down. The reason you need to be reminded so much is the same reason you read about at the beginning of this chapter about us having an undesirable quality of putting tension blocks in ourselves.

These tension blocks creep up a lot, so when you hear "heels down" that is a sign that you are tense and blocking yourself. So, relax down into your seat and legs!

Your lower legs should be on the vertical (straight up and down) line when you look from the front or back. When this is not done, it means you are not relaxing your leg on the horse, and your hip joints are not relaxed.

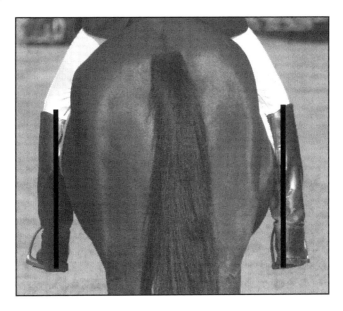

Your lower leg also needs to be in constant contact with the horse. Do you think this means stiff uncomfortable poles pushing into your horse? No, of course not. Your legs need to "breathe" with the horse. Keep them in contact, but let them move with your horse's motion. They should always be ready to aid the horse when needed.

Shoulders and Elbows

Student Emma, age 6 (riding PL Looking Glass) showing exemplary shoulders and elbows even in her young age. Photo by Leslie Hodgson.

The shoulders are a very common place for tension to be held. We can LITERALLY hold it there, keeping the muscles tense and not "letting go". Letting this continue would cause everything else in our form to be incorrect. For example, if we are holding the tension in our shoulders, that means we are not letting all of our weight rest into our seat and legs. Having tense shoulders can also inhibit our movement with the horse. Train your shoulders to relax and let the tension slide away, while the weight of your shoulders goes down to your elbows and seat.

When we are traveling straight, our shoulders should be straight and back and relaxed. It is only when we turn that our shoulders are **slightly** different, but NEVER collapse them. Your shoulders are always supposed to be PARALLEL to the horse's shoulders. To ride the horse on curved lines (circles, serpentines, etc) you must THINK OF turning your whole upper body IN from the waist. Again, don't collapse your shoulders, just ever so slightly "twist" them. POINT where you want to go. Get the feeling of your shoulders staying up and coming around (all the while staying supple).

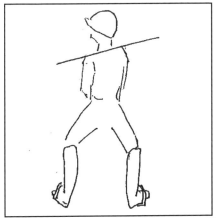

Incorrect: Collapsed Shoulders at a Turn

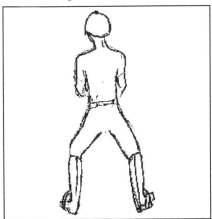

Correct Shoulders at a Turn

Elbows are tricky though an important part of riding correctly. To stay sitting up tall and in the horse's center of gravity and connected to him in everyway possible—we must keep our elbows at our side. They need to be bent, at our side, pointy and heavy. Way of thinking: Imagine connecting your seat and hips to the bit by the elbows. Ride the horse through your elbows.

Hands and Wrists

Student Katie, age 9 showing exemplary hands and wrists. Photo by Leslie Hodgson.

Your hands need to be even and held at the same height. Remember again the "straight line": Elbow, Hand, Bit. If you hold your hands to high, or too low, you break that line, and that disrupts your communication with the horse. See pictures below.

They must be held vertically, thumbs on top. This is to keep the bones in our arms from twisting, hindering our motion with the horse. Refer back to page 97.

When the hand is held correctly it can be sensitive and inviting to the horse's movements. It can create a perfect connection from your seat (the control center) to the horse's mouth. The hand must be "quiet". This means that it is not bumping and jerking around. Quiet does not necessarily mean "still". It should be still EXCEPT for the motion it makes with the horse's mouth.

Your hands are an active, living part of your riding. This does not mean that they need to fiddle or fuss. It just means that they act in accordance with your aids, and what your horse needs to hear from you.

Seek to create hands that are independent from your body. Do not post with your hands. Your hands and your elbows belong to the horse. Have them be soft and accepting of the horse's energies.

Each hand is to remain on the corresponding side of the horse's neck. "Crossing over" your hands causes you to lean incorrectly over the horse's back. The instinct to cross over is somewhat correct, but think to get the results you desire with your legs instead of your reins. Using your reins to turn you only **slightly** draw your hand **and elbow** hand BACK (not out) as if over your hip.

Head and Eyes

Student Shale, age 10 (riding PL Looking Glass), Photo by Leslie Hodgson

Our heads are a very heavy part of our body. It is because of this reason that babies cannot hold up their heads by themselves. They must build up the their neck muscles. We now have those muscles and must USE THEM to hold our head upright, like carrying a book on your head. You can throw of your entire balance if you tilt your head to either side or hang it forward or back.

Avoid tipping your head to either side, especially around curved lines. Look out and over the horse's head.

Be "noble" and dignified with your head. A proud rider creates a proud horse! If your head is hanging, you are looking down. Looking down is a very common mistake in horseback riding. Remember, we are to be visionaries—planning each step the horse takes! If we are looking down, how can we know if our circle was round? LOOK UP! Plan ahead. Know where you want to go and go there!

If we are always staring at our horse or at the ground, we cannot FEEL like we should. Riding is about feeling, communicating through nuances and aiding. TRUST the horse and look up. You will feel fantastic and free.

The back of your head should be stretched up and forward to the sky, like a string is attached to it. This also draws your chin in, fills the 'nape' of your neck and keeps your ear above your shoulder where it should be. Stretching up through the back of your head will help your whole spine and posture, making you a joy for your horse to carry.

PUTTING IT ALL TOGETHER

Stretch Up, Weight Down

Connect Your Seat Bones and Front Bones (Triangle) to the Saddle

Evenly Distribute Your Weight on Your Triangle and Stirrups

Stretch Up, Weight Down

Straight Line #1: Ear, Shoulder, Hips, Heel

Straight Line # 2: Elbow, Hand, Bit

Stretch Up, Weight Down

Soft and Movable Hips

Wrists Straight, Thumbs on Top

Open Front Line: Open, Stretched, Free, Independent

Closed and Snug Knee

Stirrups on Ball of Foot and HEEL DOWN

Stretch Up, Weight Down

Lower Legs in Contact with the Horse's Sides

Straight and Even Shoulders

Hands at Same Height and Reins at Same Length

LOOK UP!!!

Stretch Up Through the Back of Your Head, Weight Down

Let's Ride!
Let the Good Times Roll!

Aiding

What is interesting about horses is the more you do, the less they listen. So, in reverse, the less you do, the more they listen.

Moving away from pressure is something that a horse is taught to do from the time they are a foal. Watch a mare running side by side with her foal. When she wants to turn, she pushes her weight into the foal. The newborn foal might bump up against her, then realizes that his mommy is coming over, so he better move! He turns and she follows. As the foal gets older there isn't any bumping into mom anymore. He has learned so well, and can now tune in to the slightest shift in his mom's weight. They seem to be connected by an invisible cord, staying perfectly together as they turn. It is almost as if they are floating through the air like a flock of birds.

Foals are also taught this when they are halter broke. They learn that when they feel a pull on their halter, if they move back it gets tighter, and if they move forward it loosens up. We can easily teach horses to be lead by a halter because, just like the mare teaches her foal—we can develop the instinctive behavior they have to move away from pressure.

Horses, just like any creature, want to be comfortable. This is why we must make OUR way the path of least resistance. It must be EASY and COMFORTABLE for them to obey our aids. Obeying our requests should be rewarding.

Just like the mare and foal, our aiding and riding can get to the point where the horse begins to read us like a book. It is amazing how much they can feel us, and know what we are thinking right as we think it.

Amber Shaklan (Shaklans Padron NA x Bint Sihlouete)
and her 2000 foal Magnified LC (x Magnum Psyche) Photo by Leslie Hodgson

The Aiding Formula

To reach this state of "reading each other's minds", there is a formula to follow which is: "the aiding formula". It is a very simple formula but means the world to harmonious riding. It is this:

Give an aid,
get a response,
stop giving the aid.

Even more simply put:
ASK, RECEIVE, REWARD.

ASK: Know what you want, and the best way to ask for it. Ask with kindness. Know your horse and his current "mood". The pressure and length of the aid might have to vary from day to day, and from horse to horse. Every horse is different. Each day is different. Ask as quietly as you can, then if help from an artificial aid is needed, or you need to "speak" just a little louder, it is ok. You should just always seek to talk as quietly as possible to your horse through aiding. Give him the "benefit of the doubt". TRUST HIM. Give him the chance to do what you desire with the least amount of aiding that is possible.

RECEIVE: This of course is the reason why we gave the aid in the first place, to get a response. The aiding must not cease until you get the response. A horse will never learn if you do not follow through with getting the response you desire. To actually get the response, make sure you are always setting small attainable goals. If you want to go across the center to change directions, break that down into small aids. First, turn left... (reward). Then, go straight... (reward). Then, turn right... (reward).

REWARD: The greatest reward you can ever give a horse is to stop giving the aid. Remember, make what you want the horse to do the most comfortable thing. Your attitude of neutrality (being soft and quiet) IS comfortable to the horse. You MUST give the reward instantly after the response. This is the only way to "condition" the horse's responses and get him to "read your mind" like we talked about earlier.

You can always stroke the horse and use a voice reassurance when needed. Though, because this formula should be going on constantly (but invisibly)—it might be wise not to stroke or say "good boy" every single time. These rewards can be used at the end, sometime in the middle, or just when you asked for a big task and the horse performed. After the ride is a great time to give your horse a hug and thank him for his cooperation.

More About Aiding:
The word AID means: TO HELP. When we help, we must not force things, but if we don't do enough, we are hardly helping! Aids are how we talk to the horse. The horse can not understand English. Too often new riders try to verbalize what they want their horse to do. The horse does not understand, "go" or "stop". We must communicate to them through aids.

Our Tools for Aiding
SEAT (WEIGHT):
Our weight and seat bones need to be used smartly and responsibly. Plainly put, if we drop more weight into our inside seat bone, the horse will turn that way to seek to stay in balance. Weight aids are all about the horse's desire to be balanced. (more about weight aids in higher levels)

LEGS
Most of our aiding needs to come from the lower leg, and for small children, your heel. Applying the formula of ask, receive

and reward with our legs will get the horse to go forward into a faster speed with the lightest squeeze. To "steer with your legs", remember the moving away from pressure concept. If someone came to poke you in the ribs on your right side, you would move away to the left. It is the same with the horse. To turn LEFT, use RIGHT LEG. To turn RIGHT, use LEFT LEG.

REINS/BIT

The reins and the bit are to be used so that they become the horse's friend. AT NO TIME should they EVER be used for punishment. There have been plenty of horses who are afraid of the bit and any contact with it because of such abuse.

Please, always guide your horse gently. Have soft, forgiving hands that speak to the horse and say "come to me".

For steering, the rein aids are to come SECONDARY to the leg aids. For stopping, the rein aids are to come SECONDARY after the seat. Always think of your reins AFTER you have used your other aids first.

VERBAL REINFORCEMENT:

Through the aiding formula, the horse is also taught to respond to sounds such as a "cluck" or a "kiss". We can also say "whoa" to stop the horse and saying "good boy" or "good girl" is a much loved reward for the horse.

ARTIFICIAL AIDS:

These include spurs and whips. Do not cringe at the sound of those two words. They are only used to sharpen the horse's response to the natural aids. At no point should they ever be used to punish or to take out aggression or any thing of the sort on the horse.

Training & "Conditioning"

Leslie riding Gemstone LC, April 2013 Photo by designingbuzz.com

We have learned about the nature of horses and about their instincts. Now we can learn how we can use our knowledge for training the horses so our rides and time around them is more enjoyable and successful.

It is important to remember and appreciate the horse's "wondrous generosity". This animal, that is a prey animal, has agreed to let us, predators, form a partnership with them. They can learn to trust us. They look for a leader in us. Then they seek to impress and please us. It truly is amazing and heartwarming.

Let us honor them by always seeking training methods that will enhance their beauty and nature. "Training" them according to their natures is a very easy thing to do. It is all done by four training ingredients.

First Ingredient: CONDITIONING

In training, we can use the horse's natural instincts to create a language that both of us can speak and understand. You already know some of the language... it is our aiding. Most of our aids that are given are to get the horse to MOVE—forward, back, sideways, around... etc. Moving is what a horse does best. They are conditioned by nature to "flee" from danger and to always be on the move.

To accomplish getting the horse responding to the aids we give them, we have to CONDITION them. What does conditioning mean? Well, for example, we weren't born knowing the alphabet but we were conditioned to look at a letter and then put a sound to that letter. Then, we learned how to put those letters and sounds together to form WORDS. Then, and only then, could we read and write sentences!

In the same way, we must teach the horse: "this aid means 'go'"; "this aid means 'turn'". Then, we can say "go" and "turn" at the same time. And THEN, we can say "go at exactly this speed and then turn here in a small circle, and then turn the other way in a small circle going at this different speed". That is taking letters, then making words and then sentences.

Second Ingredient: REWARDING

A reward is to encourage the horse to respond in the exact same way the next time that the EXACT SAME aid is given. How do we reward? Rewarding is in the third and final part of our aiding formula "stop giving the aid". By going back to neutral and letting ourselves and the horse rest into the new direction, speed, or gait that they just gave us as a response to our aid, we are reaffirming to the horse that, "YES, that is what I want."

You can also reward the horse in other ways: small strokes, a reassuring voice, and other affectionate things.

Third Ingredient: TIMING

Timing is CRUCIAL to correct conditioning and rewarding. For example, if the horse doesn't respond to our leg and seat driving aids, we must INSTANTLY give him a light tap with the whip. If we don't instantly reward the horse by ceasing the aid, then he will not learn to respond to that aid.

To have correct TIMING, we need to LISTEN as hard as we can to the horse.

Only the horse can tell us WHEN and HOW MUCH. For example, one day your horse might be lazy, so more distinct or artificial aids might have to be given to get him to trot. Then that same horse the next day can have a lot of energy and the leg aid you used the day before to get him to trot might make him canter off.

You get to pick WHICH aids to use, WHERE to give them and WHERE and WHEN to go. You choose the pace. You choose the school figure.

Fourth Ingredient: REPETITION

When we are consistent and repeat the aiding formula in the same way over and over again, the horse will have a perfect knowledge and be able to respond the same way to the same aid every time. Then we can "up our requests" and repeat the formula more.

The Best Way

The best way to get the horse's cooperation and willingness is to speak POSITIVELY to him through your aids. Speaking down to anyone (horse or human) and pointing out their faults is a sure way to make them stay away from you and not want to be nice to you.

Examples: Instead of saying "Don't look over there", say

with your aids, "Look over here". Instead of saying "Stop going around the fence", say with your aids, "Jump the fence!".

It is great to think of our bodies as a bunch of individual parts that all have their own voice. They each say different things to the horse after they have been conditioned to respond to them.

Your Ride
Level One and Two

Loosening Exercises:
•   Walk on the loose rein
•   Rising trot
•   Simple, large, open school figures; round-off the corners
•   Forward and down stretching

Suppling Exercises:
•   Smaller school figures, (10m circles, tighter serpentines, deeper into the corners)
•   Frequent changes of rein
•   Lengthening and shortening the stride in trot
•   Transitions

Loosening exercises allow the horse to "settle in" and get warmed up. Before we can begin any work, the horse has to be accepting of our weight on its back. It would be rude to impose on the horse to do tight school figures when he hasn't even had a chance to stretch and get rid of his "stable stiffness".

Large school figures are to be used to get the horse loose and stretched. Forward and down stretching will encourage the horse to lift his back and carry you "elastically".

119

It is a very good idea that with each ride you start off walking on a loose rein or 'on the buckle'. Remember, a horse doesn't like to be trapped, and you don't want him to feel trapped in your hands or your seat. You always want to feel energy and motion coming from the back of the horse, under your seat and up his neck into your hands. Walking on the loose rein can inspire the horse be "be natural". It also gives you a chance to relax and mentally prepare yourself for the ride.

When you begin to trot, always rise (post). This takes a great deal of your weight off the horse's back so he can continue to stretch it and be "through". Only after your horse is good and warmed up should you practice sitting trot.

School figures help us to ride with purpose. Circles of different sizes, serpentines, changes of direction all give us a "pattern" to ride.

Having a purpose will keep the horse concentrated on his work. If you have purpose and your horse has a will, every ride will be a meaningful ride. It will be meaningful because you set yourselves up for success.

Setting Up for Success:
- Set Attainable Goals
- Be Visionary, Have a Goal in Mind
- Give Clear Aids
- Focus Attention
- Stay Emotionally Detached
- Use Correct Timing of Aids
- Use Encouragement and Reinforcement

The Best Way

Gift of Gold "Gracie"
and Student Lauren, Age 9.
These two are a true example of how persistence, dedication and a strong love
of horses can overcome challenges and barriers. Photo by Leslie Hodgson.

When we ride or are around horses, there are obviously going to be times where everything doesn't go perfectly. There are several instances where a student's confidence level will soar high until something happens that makes them realize that horses aren't angels all the time. Then, they start to get nervous.

It is important in our horse business and for life in general to be able to overcome our frustrations and our fears. We need to be able to say, "You know what? There is a solution to any problem and I am going to find it. I am going to be brave and face the situation."

Being the Trusted Leader

If the horse gets frightened and shies or bolts, our reactions and attitude towards the horse should be calm and "detached". We will talk more about detaching in a moment.

We need to stay calm in order to keep the horse being confident in us. It would be very wrong to pull on the horse's mouth angrily or to yell and scream and get all spooked ourselves. This would only confirm in the horse's mind that there really IS something to be afraid of!

Instead, we should ignore whatever the horse spooked about or is afraid of and encourage the horse to go forward. We must let the horse feel that we are not scared or upset at all, and by so doing, will calm the horse down. It really is a mind game with the horse. We cannot confirm in their minds that there is a reason to be scared. If we are calm and encourage the horse to be calm as well, we will eventually get that horse to trust more in us and do what we demand of them.

When Should Punishment Be Used?

Horses resent demonstrations of authority. They will mentally "turn off" if we decide to get authoritative and "bossy".

Most discipline is rarely understood by horses, because most discipline rarely involves a consideration of how horses think. If we but learn how a horse thinks, and we strive to use the right methods, we can always achieve the behaviors we want.

In most cases, it is the miscommunication of the rider that has caused the problems. Are you too stiff in your body or your mind? Did you give clear aids? Are you asking the horse to do something he isn't ready for yet? Did you lose your focus while handling and get clumsy and startle your horse?

If punishment IS needed in extremely rare cases, think instead in terms of CORRECTION. Correction is to be done assertively, (not aggressively), swiftly, and with a clear, understandable purpose. Then, it is done. Do not hold grudges and try to "get back" at the horse. Doing this would be simply preposterous because the horse WILL NOT understand unless you made your point right in or directly after the undesired act.

Our Opportunity

The reason so many people punish horse's unfairly is because of their own lack of self-control and their ill temper.

We have been given a great opportunity through horses to teach ourselves. We can learn to curb our temper and control our emotions. Sometimes it might seem like the horse is out to get you. This is never the case. If a horse is angry, it is because of the way it has been raised, trained and treated.

So, practice self-control around horses. Train yourselves to stay calm in situations where the horse isn't calm. This comes back to the word "detaching". Detach means "to separate from".

What do we need to separate from?
• Our instinct to react in fright or anger
• Our emotions: When we are frightened, angry, upset or nervous... the horse will sense those emotions. What is scarier than an angry tiger to a horse?

How Do We Detach?

This concept is a life-long process to master. So many people react instantly to what they are feeling. This is called being irrational. It IS OK to have feelings and to feel angry, upset or frightened. They are natural human emotions. We should always address the issue and get it resolved.

The point of the above paragraphs is that we should not do it to or on the horse. It is not fair to them. They have no concept of people insulting each other or anything else that might upset us. They do not know our personal ambitions. We cannot tell it to them. All they can do is FEEL. For this reason, horses are amazing. They are one of the best tools that we have on this earth to teach us how to control our emotions and our tempers.

Practicing Self Control

It is easy to be calm and be able to correct the horse fairly when we ourselves are calm and happy. It becomes more difficult when we ourselves are frightened or upset. This is when we must practice self control.

When we are in a bad mood, it is easy to overreact about what the horse is doing. It's like when we have a headache and all of the sudden everything SOUNDS louder and LOOKS brighter and people seem to be out to just annoy you. In reality, the people around us are not being randomly louder one day, the sun did not get brighter and the world isn't out to get us... it just seems that way because WE aren't our normal selves.

So, don't make the mistake of punishing the horse when they SEEM to be spooking more or not being as soft and round today as they were yesterday if you yourself are upset. Just be rational!

A Look into "Attitudes"

Passive

Another reason people might get into conflicts with horses is because people are too PASSIVE. A leader cannot be passive. Passive means that you stand there and let everything happen around you, even if you don't like it and you know it's wrong. An example of a passive person would be someone who lets their friends talk them into doing something they know is wrong. Another example of a passive person would be someone who lets somebody treat them wrongly.

An example of a passive rider is one who lets their horse treat them unfairly by running over the top of them. Or one who lets their horse go whatever speed they decide. Or one who repeatedly lets their horse go around a jump or lets them walk as far as they want to away from an obstacle that they are spooked about.

Aggressive

The best way to describe and aggressive person is to think of a bully. Everybody listens to the bully because they'll get beat up if they don't... but everybody hates the bully and is afraid of him. The bully will never have people doing nice things for him just because they want to. Nobody wants to serve someone who is rude and demanding.

An aggressive rider would be one who says to their horse by spurring and whipping irrationally "You dumb horse! You didn't go over that fence and now you are going to pay!" Or one who says, "You are making me so mad!" The aggressive rider blames everything on the horse.

Assertive

This is our ultimate goal. It is not even a mix between being passive or aggressive... it is its own attitude. An example of an assertive person is a great leader that people love and respect. A great leader gets the most accomplished with the best results. Why? Because they know how to communicate. They know how to get people's respect. The passive person receives no respect because he never stands up for what he believes in. The aggressive person receives no respect because he demands it out of people, and if they don't give it, he hurts them either physically or emotionally.

An assertive person gets respect simply by not being passive, or aggressive. To be an assertive person we must stand up for what we believe in. We cannot put up with ill treatment. We must respect others by not ever hurting them physically or emotionally.

An assertive rider says to their horse by encouragement and clear aids, "It wasn't ok to refuse that jump. Let's go back and get over it this time." An assertive rider rides with this conversation in mind while doing the proper aids to communicate it to the horse, "Oh, nope, that is a little too fast, slow down. Good job, you listened! Oh, now we are getting a little too slow, go on. Hey, you aren't listening. There you go! Good boy!"

With this assertive attitude of giving and receiving respect from our horse, we might be surprised at how willing the horse is to try harder and harder for us. They get rewarded every time they are "going right" by having a quiet, happy rider on their backs. They also are not confused because when they do something that does not please the rider, the rider lets them know clearly and quickly and then forgives them, forgets and moves on! Who wouldn't want to be led by a leader like that?

We all probably do little things wrong every day. Most likely, so will our horse. It would not be fun to be yelled and screamed at OR to not have anybody ever tell you what you are doing wrong. Our ultimate goal is to keep getting better and better and to make the horse better and better each day. Be the same kind of leader to your horse that you would want to lead you to become a better person.

An assertive person and rider know that only they are in control of their attitude. No one can MAKE them mad.

As an assertive person and rider, we are in complete control of ourselves and our horse. We are keeping a great partnership alive between us and the horse because we are communicating effectively and being a strong leader. We aren't letting the horse do whatever he wants especially when it's wrong... but we aren't punishing him unjustly either.

Continue practicing being a great leader in your partnership with your horse by controlling your emotions and being assertive.

*Stay dedicated and loyal to your
horse and to your riding progression.*

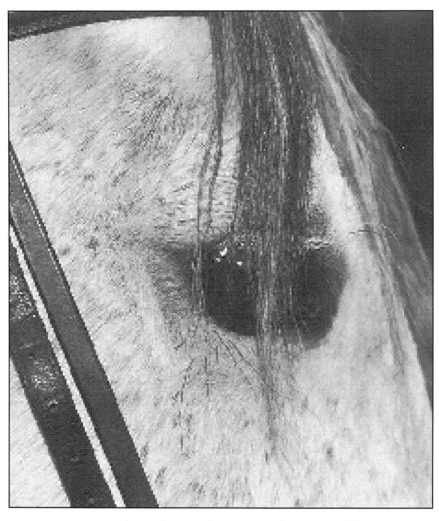

*Be patient, kind, understanding, willing and
dignified and let those qualities radiate
through you and your horse.*

MWF Izabella (VF Premonition x OKW Iviore, by Bandos) Photo by Leslie Hodgson

Section 4
Horsemanship

Student Rachael, age17 with Prairie Fire V, Photo by Leslie Hodgson

Leslie's daughter Launa with Spirit, Photo by Leslie Hodgson

Do you truly love the horse? Do you feel personal joy when you know your horse is happy? Do you feel inspired to reaffirm your dedication to your horse everyday?

These are the true feelings of horsemanship. You cannot just ride. If you care about the horse, you will learn to care for him. We, as horsemen and horsewomen have a very large responsibility. Our horses need us. They depend on us for their food, shelter, and health.

How cruel it would be to be inconsiderate of all our horses needs. We need to learn what they need, how much they need—or don't need, and how and when to give it to them.

General Maintenance

Bay Balou (Huckleberry Bey x Baskazelle), Photo by Leslie Hodgson

Feeding:

Even though we have a large variety of feed available for horses, it is important to remember that they are a grazing animal. Horses are herbivores and foragers by nature. Your horse's diet needs to be primarily made of roughage (grass or hay). Keeping hay and or grass in front of them as much as possible, makes for very happy and healthy horses. Of course, it is not always possible to do so, but you can be sure to satisfy their urge to chew and give them the nutrients they need by providing high quality hay.

HAY:

The bulky part of the horse's diet is called roughage. There are two different kind of roughage: fresh—like grass, and preserved—like hay. Hay is dried grass and it falls into two categories: Legume Hay and Grass Hay

Legume Hay:

Two examples of legume hay are Alfalfa and Clover. Alfalfa is more commonly seen than clover hay. It is very green and leafy, It is a great mineral source that is very high in protein... (sometimes too much for some horses). Its leaves are more plentiful and larger than other grasses. It is very rich. If you choose to feed Alfalfa, always feed less of it than you would grass hay.

Grass Hay:

Grass hay is generally lower in protein and energy. It is also higher in fiber. This it what makes grass hay an excellent choice for horses. This is because you can feed more of it to satisfy your horse's appetite without over feeding calories and protein.

Hay Evaluation:

Good hay is crisp, smells sweet and is green/greenish-brown in color. It has very fine stems, and is as leafy as possible. It should be soft when you touch it. Bad quality hay has little nutritional value, and if it is old, it can be moldy, which can cause colic. Bad hay is yellowish-brown, and has more stalk than leaf. It is very sun bleached and smells moldy, musty and/or dusty. You should also avoid hay that has weeds, dirt and trash.

GRAIN:

Grain is what we call concentrated feeds. There is a very large variety of concentrated feed available.

- Coarse Mix: this is a mixture of oats, corn and some pellets. It takes longer to eat which might be desirable to some horse own-
   ers.
- Oats: This feed has low energy contents. It is popular because you can make careless changes to the amount you give, and it makes little nutritional difference. It is easy to feed!
- Bran: Bran is most commonly used in a "mash" (mixed with

hot water). It is a bulk food, not a main source of nutrition. Young horses do not do well with bran, because it doesn't have enough calcium for them.

- Flaked Corn: Corn has a lot of nutritional value. It is often mixed with oats.
- Pellets: There are many different pellets to meet very different needs of each horse and owner. Pellets are great for this reason. Feed companies make different nutritional contents for different reasons. Buy the right one for your horse.
- Alfalfa Pellets: Just like the hay, these pellets are a high source of vitamins and minerals. It is very valuable for its calcium and fiber content. Because of this, and its easiness to eat, it is most commonly used for older horses.
- Barley: Very high energy content. Take care in feeding it.
- Beet Pulp: This is dried beet and must be soaked before eat ing. It is another feed that is rich in energy and protein, good for horses that need "bulking".

How Much to Feed:

How much you feed your horse depends on each individual. Horses at different ages and stages of growth have different needs. Horses at different work loads and activity have different dietary needs as well. Just like people, horses have different metabolisms.

Watering:

Normally, horses drink about 5 gallons a day. Most times, horses will drink even more during the summer months when it is hot outside. If your horse does not have access to water he could be in danger of dehydration, heat exhaustion, choking, and even colic. Imagine how it feels to be without water. We should never have to put our horse in that predicament. Water is easy to give!

Weight Evaluation

The best way to tell how much your horse needs is to evaluate his weight at least once a week. Watch him and adjust his weight accordingly. Try to find the amount he needs, and remember to split up the grain to 2 times a day, and the hay 3-5 times a day.

How to tell if your horse is too thin or too overweight:

POOR: Extremely thin; spine protrudes very far; ribs and hip bones project prominently; tailhead has extremely visible "individual vertebrae"; no fatty tissue can be seen or felt.

VERY THIN: Thin; slight fatty covering over base of spine; spine protrudes, ribs, tailhead, and hip bones project prominently. Withers, neck and shoulders have very slight muscle and fatty structure.

THIN: Fat buildup about halfway on spinal column; slight fat covering over ribs; spinal processes and ribs can be easily seen, but are slightly "filled" in by fat; tailhead prominent, but individual vertebrae cannot be seen visually; withers, shoulders, and neck accentuated.

MODERATELY THIN: Slight ridge along back; ribs not as easily seen, but for a faint outline; tailhead prominence depends on conformation; fat can begin to be felt around it; withers, shoulders and neck not obviously thin.

MODERATE: Back is flat (no crease or ridge); cannot see ribs, but can easily feel them with your fingers; around tailhead and area beginning to feel "spongy"; withers appear rounded over spinal processes; shoulders and neck blend smoothly into body.

MODERATELY FLESHY: May have slight crease down back; fat over ribs spongy; fat around tailhead soft; fat beginning to be deposited along the side of withers, behind shoulders, and along sides of neck.

FLESHY: May have crease down back; individual ribs can be felt, but noticeable filling between ribs with fat; fat around tailhead soft; fat deposited along withers, behind shoulders and along neck.

FAT: Crease down back; difficult to feel ribs; fat around tailhead very soft; area along withers filled with fat; area behind shoulder filled with fat; noticeable thickening of neck; fat deposited along inner thighs.

EXTREMELY FAT: Obvious crease down back; patchy fat appearing over ribs; bulging fat around tailhead, along withers, behind shoulders, and along neck; flank filled with fat.

Weight Gain Regime: To get your horse's weight "up" can be done different ways, and it NEEDS to be done different ways for each horse's situation. Some horses might need to be wormed very bad, but doing so could cause a lot of other body disfunctions. Each horse that is thin needs to be worked up GRADUALLY. You can do the horse more harm than good putting him in a big grass pasture or starting to feed him large amounts of food. The horse that is thin either has a disease or sickness, or is not getting enough to eat. In any case, his system is accustomed to his condition, and he needs to be worked into another body condition slowly.

Weight Loss Regime: Weight reduction is a slow steady process so it doesn't stress your horse out. Gradually increase horse's exercising. Use restraint in feeding your horse. Bring his grain down slowly, to very minimal or no rations. Switch or reduce amount of alfalfa hay. Replace with a mature grass hay. Feed separate from other horses so the overweight horse doesn't eat his neighbor's portion. In extreme cases of obesity, reduce or terminate your horse's pasture intake. This is to keep him safe from sicknesses caused by obesity.

Dangers of obesity:
- Stress on heart and lungs
- Greater risk of laminitis or founder
- More strain on feet, joints and limbs
- Makes arthritis worse
- Growing young horses can get developmental diseases in their legs and joints
- Harder to cool down
- Fat build up around key organs
- Makes for a lazy and easily tuckered-out horse!

Exercising
Conditioning, Warm-Up, Cool-Down, Turn-Out

Our horses are athletes. We ask them to perform duties with us on their backs, and often times, we ask them to do it with beauty and grace. Do you think all the people that compete at the Olympics just woke up one day and were ready to compete for the gold medal? No, of course not. Marathon runners and sprinters, ice skaters, gymnasts, swimmers, and many more all spend years preparing for the big event!

These athletes slowly condition themselves, stepping up their work gradually. They challenge themselves in their work, but do not "over-do" it. This way, they can progress quickly without getting injured. They know that each of their muscles, tendons and bones are very important so they do proper stretching and warm-up exercises every single time they are going to practice or "work-out". Then, after their practice or work-out they stretch again to cool down which minimizes the chance for cramping and tight, sore muscles.

They eat right, and they get the required amount of sleep. They stick to their work and eating schedules. The end result is something beautiful. Those people are amazing what they do, aren't they?

We need to be just as concerned about our horses muscles, tendons, joints and bones. We must be concerned, because we are in control of our ride. The horse will do what we ask him to do. Let us be considerate of the horse and help him become a great athlete.

WARM UP:
Always begin your ride with a proper warm-up. Don't overwork your horse. Make sure you give him little walking breaks in between. To get him conditioned to be able to take on a big long ride, for pleasure or for competition, step up his work gradually. If it is gradual enough, moving up their work in increments of 4-5 days or a week would give the horse a chance to get accustomed to the increase he was asked to make, and then, only then, can you move it up again.

COOL DOWN:
Cool down is very important to the horse for the same reason it is to the Olympic athlete—to avoid cramping and soreness. A horse is cooled down when his breathing is back to normal and he has either cooled to the touch, or his sweat has dried. These signs would alert you that his respiratory rate is back to normal.

You can cool down your horse in different (but much the same) ways: walking on the loose rein on his back or walking him in hand or on a hot-walker after you have un-tacked. Be sure not to let him gulp cold water, or eat any grain until he is fully cooled. This would cause the infamous stomach cramps. Your horse may have small sips of luke-warm water, but usually, they can just wait until their breathing has slowed and their bodies have cooled.

If possible, it is very important that your horse gets turn out. Even 2-3 hours in a paddock would suffice. Some horses are very lucky and get to be out in pastures all day long. Turn-out is important because horses love to move around and graze. It keeps their muscles moving so they don't get stiff, and it keeps food in their bellies. There are plenty of considerations in deciding where to turn out your horse—like the amount of grass your horse should eat for weight purposes, and if they get along with other horses or not. Turn out, at least a couple times a week, is essential because it will keep them happy and fresh.

Shoeing/Trimming

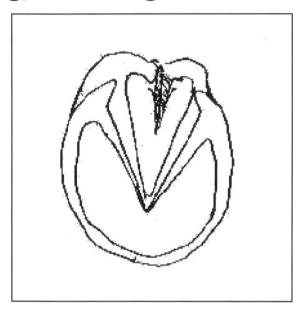

A horse's hooves are just like our finger and toe nails... they grow! So, just like with our nails, a horse's hooves must be trimmed regularly too. Every 6-8 weeks is the standard time between farrier visits.

There is a famous saying that says, "No hoof, no horse!" How true that is. If our horse has unhealthy feet, he cannot do anything normally. Letting the horse get long feet is cruel and dangerous. Some neglected horse's feet get so long, they start curling upwards. That takes a very long time of very frequent and thoughtful farrier visits to correct, while the horse is in pain the whole time.

If the horse has shoes on they need to get reset every 6-8 weeks as well. If the horse's hooves are left too long without getting trimmed when they have shoes on, the horse can pull the shoe off and risk injuring himself in many ways, or the hoof will begin to grow over the shoe. So, again, every 6-8 weeks this should be done.

Worming

Horses are constantly exposed to worms. When grazing in a pasture, they cannot avoid it. Worm eggs are everywhere. For our domesticated horses, who are kept in small areas, the amount of worms they ingest can be fatal. Wild horses rarely ever develop a worm infestation severe enough to be fatal because they are constantly moving over a wide area.

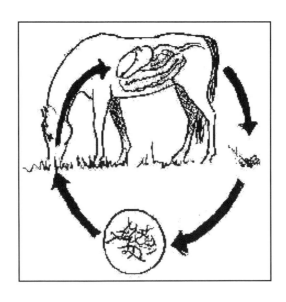

Life-cycle of the worm:

Worm eggs hatch and the larvae climb up the grass stalks which is then eaten by the horse. The larvae grow inside the horse until they are adults. Then the adult worms release eggs which eventually come out in the horse's manure. The manure breaks down and then the eggs hatch again and climb up the grass stalks.

There will always be worm eggs and for this reason, we must consistently de-worm about every 6-8 weeks. There are also daily dewormers available that are consistently in the horse's digestive tract, and help to kill the larvae. Even when the horse is on this supplement, they still need to be dewormed every 6-8 weeks.

There are many kinds of wormer. The most popular are Strongid and Ivermectin. They can come in a paste, or a liquid. Most common and easy for you are the paste tubes.

How to give wormer:

1) Adjust the appropriate weight dosage for your horse.

2) Stand on the side and put your arm around his nose.

3) Insert the tube gently into the corner of his mouth & push the end of the tube so the wormer comes out.

4) Keep the horse's head up so they swallow the paste instead of spitting it out.

Vaccinating

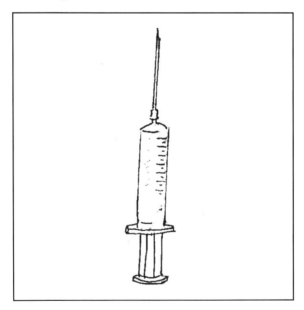

Shots keep your horse safe from diseases. Common vaccinations to give to all horses in any region are influenza (flu), equine viral rhinopneumonitis (rhino), and tetanus.

DISEASES/VACCINATIONS:

Flu: Viral infection that makes the horse's respiratory tract irritated, causing coughing for weeks after recovery. Give every 6 months, in the spring if your horse lives in a closed herd of currently vaccinated horses. More often (perhaps every three months) if your horse travels or commingles with other groups.

Rhino: Same as above. This vaccination is given according to your vets recommendations.

Tetanus: Usually fatal disease caused by bacteria. Risk is high with horses that aren't vaccinated. Give 1x per year.

Rabies: Viral disease that is fatal. Spread by bite or saliva of infected mammals. Any animal (including you) are at risk when around an affected animal. This shot is given 1x a year, in the spring.

There are always other geographically orientated diseases and new ones showing up all the time. Ask your vet to keep you informed and purchase any shots you need to protect your animals. Examples are: Strangles, West Nile Virus, Potomac Horse Fever, etc.

Young horses might need to get vaccinated more often. Again, talk to your veterinarian about a vaccination schedule for your horse(s).

Dental Care:
Floating

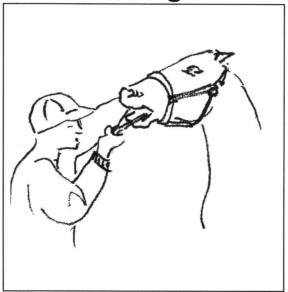

Floating removes sharp enamel points from your horse's teeth which keeps them smooth and even. The horse gets these sharp edges from the sideways motion in which they chew, and the soft feed that they eat which doesn't give their teeth a big enough "work out" to keep them filed down.

When their teeth are not smooth and even, your horse can suffer in many ways: • Pain. Showed by head tilting or tossing; bit chewing; fighting the bit or resisting the bridle. • Health and appearance: body condition falls, gets thinner. • Trouble eating: difficulty chewing, drops food from mouth, excessive saliva.

Keep in mind that some horses might not show any of these signs simply because horses get used to feeling uncomfortable. Periodic dental exams are highly recommended to keep happy, healthy horses. Dental exams should be done by your vet because it requires feeling inside the horse's mouth. You can learn to feel the teeth if your vet chooses to teach you.

To float a horse, your vet will file down your horse's molars with a metal "rasp". Your horse will probably not like it at all, but will feel much better afterwards!! Most vets use sedation to do dental procedures. This is to help keep everybody safe from getting hurt.

Seasonal Care:
Summer Care vs. Winter Care

Horses have very different needs for the different seasons. Both summer and winter have about the same amount of work though!

Summer:
- More water
- Fly control
- Sunburn control
- Botfly egg removal
- Dust control
- Spring: observance of weight increase risk, end of summer when grass dies: weight loss risk.
- Hoof moisturizer to prevent cracking

Winter:
- Unfreezing water
- More feed (usually)
- Blanketing
- Mud control
- Rain rot risk observance
- If in stall more: picking of feet to prevent abscesses and thrush.

Normal Vital Signs—
What They Are & How to Check

Knowing these by heart is a great tool for knowing what to do and look for with a horse you think is sick or injured.

Temperature: 99-101.5 degrees Fahrenheit. Below normal can mean hypothermia or shock. Above normal can mean infection and heat exhaustion, exercise or muscle exertion.

Heart Rate: 30-44 beats per minute. Below normal can mean a heart problem, poisoning, hypothermia, shock, good athletic condition. Above normal can mean they are exercising, in pain, have a fever, heat exhaustion, shock, heart problem, anxiety.

Respiratory Rate: 10-15 breaths per minute. Below normal means hypothermia, shock or drug effect. Above normal can mean they are exercising, in pain, have a fever, heat exhaustion, shock, electrolyte imbalance or a respiratory infection.

Gut Sounds: Long, rolling rumbles with short gurgles, quite periods no longer than two minutes. Quieter than normal means colic or illness. Noisier than normal means they are digesting their meal, are hungry or they could be nervous or have gut inflammation. High-pitched "pings" with periods of quiet is a sign of accumulated gas, often associated with colic.

Digital Pulse: Subtle and Difficult to feel. No pulse could be normal or indicate poor circulation. A strong pulse that is easy   t o feel could mean your horse has laminitis or maybe an abscess.

Gum Color: Pale to bubble-gum pink. Whitish gums could mean the horse is in shock. Bright pink gums might mean your horse is ill, has been poisoned, or is in shock. This color could be normal if   your horse has just been exercising. Colors of brick-red, blue, or a muddy color   could mean your horse has poisoning or is in shock.

Capillary refill time: 1-2 seconds. Faster than usual means your horse's blood pressure is higher than usual, due to exercise, excitement or anxiety. CRT slower than usual indicates poisoning, illness, or shock.

How to check for these vital signs:
Temperature:

1) Shake down a glass thermometer or turn on an electronic one.
2) Good idea to put some kind of lubricant on the tip, like Vasaline®
3) Move the tail and gently insert the thermometer into the rectum.
4) Hold the thermometer in place. It's a good idea to stabilize your hand on the horse.
5) You can let go of the tail if the horse is irritated with you holding it.
6) With a glass thermometer, attach a string and clip to the horse's tail.
7) Glass thermometers: time 2 minutes. Electronic thermometers: about 30 seconds—listen for the beep.

Heart Rate:

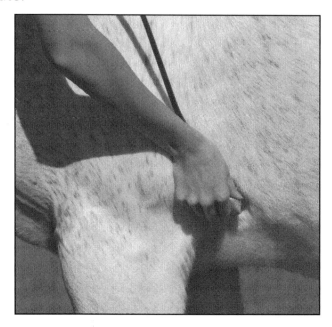

1) You need a watch with a second hand, or a digital timer.
2) Stand on the horse's left side and face his elbow.
3) Place bell of the stethoscope behind the point of his elbow and press gently into his armpit.
4) Heart beat should be "lub and dub"—count the two together as one beat.
5) Count the number of beats in a 15-second period.
6) Multiply that number by 4 for "beats per minute"

Checking Heart Rate Digitally:
1) Hold horse's halter with one hand and place the fingertips of your other hand under his jawbone beneath his cheek.
2) To find it, slide your fingers up and down the jaw bone. The artery is about half the size of a pencil.
3) When you have found it, gently feel for the pulse.
4) Count the number of beats in a 15-second period of time.
5) Multiply that number by 4 for "beats per minute".

Respiratory Rate:

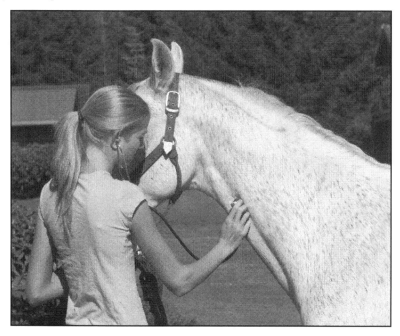

1) Place the bell of your stethoscope in the center of your horse's throat (in between the throat latch and the chest.
2) Listen to the air being inhaled and exhaled.
3) Count the number of beats in a 15-second period of time.
4) Multiply that number by 4 for "breaths per minute"

Gut Sounds:

1) Place your stethoscope on your horses belly.

2) Listen to different sections for at least 30 seconds.

3) It is important to listen for long enough, because remember that there can be quiet periods of up to two minutes.

4) Sometimes, you can hear gut sounds just pressing your ear up against the horses barrel.

Digital Pulse:

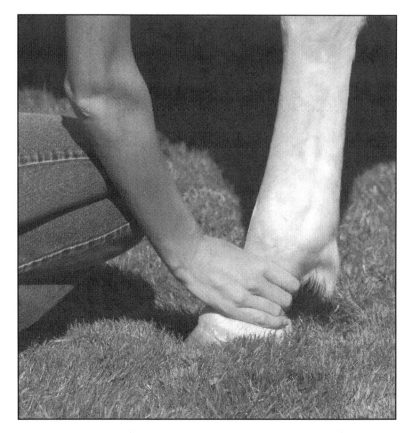

1) Squat down (do not kneel) beside your horse's front leg.
2) Place your fingertips along the outside of his pastern area
3) Feel for a pulse in that artery
4) You just feel to see if you can feel it or not, you do not need to know beats per minute in this case.

Gum Color:

1) Lift the horse's lip and look at the color

Capillary Refill Time:
1)   While lip is lifted, use a finger to press on the gums.
2)   Press so the color in that spot blanches out.
3)   Let go, then count how many seconds it takes to go back
to   the same color.

Dehydration:

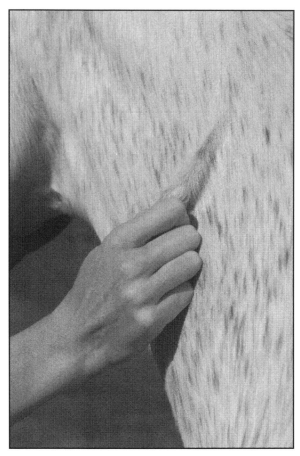

1) Look at your horse flank area, if it is sucked up and in, your horse is dehydrated.

2) Pinch a small amount of skin on the horse's neck, let go and count how many seconds it takes to shrink back to normal. If it doesn't shrink in 2 seconds or less, your horse is dehydrated.

3) If your horse is dehydrated, give him the correct dose of electrolyte powder or paste.

Sicknesses and Diseases

Colic

The first thing to know about colic is that it is the number one killer of horses. It is not a disease, it is a sickness. The term "colic" means "belly-ache". Colicing horses have a problem with their digestive system. Colic usually follows a combination of signs that let you know your horse has abdominal pain.

Colic can range from mild to severe, but should NEVER be ignored. Many of the conditions that cause your horse to colic can become life-threatening in a very short time.

THE SIGNS OF COLIC:
- Turning the head toward to flank
- Pawing
- Kicking or biting at the abdomen
- Stretching out as if to urinate, but doesn't
- Repeatedly lying down or getting up, or "pretending" like

he's going to
- Rolling, (especially violent rolling)
- Sitting in a dog-like position, or lying on the back
- Lack of bowel movements (can tell by small number of manure piles)
- Absence of, or reduced digestive ("gut") sounds
- Lack of appetite
- Putting head down to drink water, but doesn't drink
- Sweating
- Rapid Respiration and/or flared nostrils
- Elevated pulse rate (greater than 52 beats per minute)
- Depression
- Lip Curling
- Cool extremities

Taking Action:
TIME is very important to treating a colicing horse
1) Remove all food and water
2) Notify your veterinarian immediately
3) Be prepared with the following information:
   A) Pulse Rate
   B) Respiratory rate (breathing)
   C) Temperature
   D) Gum color
   E) Capillary refill time... gum color
   F) Behavioral signs (what is your horse acting like?)
   G) Digestive noises, or lack of them
   H) Bowel movements: what color?, how often?, what firmness?
   I) Know his routine and if it has changed recently
   J) Health records: including deworming and any past episodes of colic.
4) Keep horse calm and comfortable (as much as possible). Allow the horse to lie down, unless he is at risk of injuring himself (but don't enter the stall if he will injure you!)

5) If he is behaving violently, attempt to walk him around slowly
6) No drugs for pain, unless your vet tells you otherwise
7) Make sure you follow your vet's instructions exactly and wait for him/her to get there.

Your vet will do a number of things, depending on the severity of the colic. He will examine the horse and ask you a lot of questions about the horse's history to identify the cause. Then he might do a variety of things such as: put a stomach tube in the horse, rectal palpation, blood test, abdominal tap, give him sedatives to relieve pain and distress, give him laxatives to get the intestines working correctly again, watch him to see his reaction to the treatments, and if already severe or if the horse is not responding he will send him to a veterinarian clinic to get surgery.

Causes and Preventions
We do have the potential to reduce and control colic—the number one killer of horses. Colic can result from a few different incidences that all affect the horse's digestive tract. Here is a quick list of CAUSES and PREVENTIONS:
• Moldy Feed. Examine your hay and grain before feeding it to your horse. It should always be fresh and devoid of mold.
• Too much grain consumption (accidently getting out and eating the whole bucket, or too much at one time.) Make sure his door is closed at night and if you have a horse that is skilled at escaping, devise a way to keep him   in. Split his rations up to at least two feedings per day.
• Not being fed enough hay (or grass), acid build-up. Horses are a grazing animal and they need food in their stomachs all the time or their stomach acid will cause ulcers. Spread out their hay rations to 3-5 times a day when they stay inside. If they are out grazing, that is enough food in their stomachs.
• Stress. Some horses are very sensitive to their routine. A change in surroundings, like being moved to a new barn and/or location (like to a show) could be stressful to some horses. Trans-

porting could be stressful also. Just know your horse and what he is susceptible to.

• Blood Poisoning. Poisonous plants can cause this. Know what they are and then survey your pastures.

• Sand/dirt consumption ("Sand Colic"). In dry climates your horse needs to be fed off the ground. Some people prefer to feed their horse off the ground all the time. Personal experience and again, knowing your horse well will help you know what to do.

• Parasites (worms). Keep your horse wormed! Parasites can cause many digestive dysfunctions.

• Being deprived of water. Sickness and stress can be caused if your horse does not have clean, fresh water when he needs it. Know how much your horse needs each day and make sure he has it.

Laminitis

Laminitis is a disease process that causes reduced blood flow to your horse's foot and then causes a breakdown of the attachments to the hoof, called the laminae. The laminae attaches the coffin bone to the hoof wall. (DIAGRAM—4 of normal hoof and mild, moderate and severe detachments, rotation of the coffin bone.)

Causes:

Although laminitis happens in the feet, the causes happen elsewhere in the body.

• Grain overload
• Obesity
• Abrupt changes in diet, and sudden access to rich grass without having time to adapt.
• High fever or illness
• "Road founder"—repeated and excessive concussion to the feet
• Severe colic
• Acute Endometrius (uterine infection)
• Endotoxemia (blood poisoning)

Other Terms:
Acute laminitis is the disease occurring in just the first couple days.
Chronic laminitis has been going on for longer than several days.
Founder signifies chronic laminitis.

How can you tell if your horse has laminitis?
• Signs of Lameness (limping, walking tender-footed and slow, hurts to turn sharp)
• Moving stiffly (as if walking on glass)
• Reluctant to move at all
• Rocking Back on Hind Feet when moving forward
• Holding his front feet out in front of his shoulders when at rest
• Pain in the toes when pinched
• Not eating
• Depressed
• Feverish
• Ate more than usual within the past couple days
• Heat in two front or all four hooves.
• Can feel a strong digital pulse on the affected feet compared to his other feet or compared to other horse's feet on the premises.

Treatment:
Laminitis is treated by stopping the breakdown process, resolving the underlying cause, and restoring circulation to the foot. The sooner in the disease process that these efforts are made, the better the outcome will be.
1) stop feeding all concentrated feeds
2) no pasture turnout—stall rest
3) only grass hay until vet says otherwise
4) other drugs prescribed by vet: antibiotics, pain relief, etc.
5) bed stalls thickly—lots of cushion
6) vet and farrier work—corrective trimming, frog supports and therapeutic shoes or pads.

Other important points: Some horses, especially if caught early recover quickly and go on normally and healthily through life. Unfortunately, some do not and have to be put down for humane reasons. It is important to remember that once your horse has had laminitis, it is very likely to happen again. If your horse has had it, managing closely his lifestyle can help prevent it from happening again.

The most important thing in preventing laminitis is to not let your horse get fat or obese and not ever letting him overdose on alfalfa hay, grain, or lush pastures. Keep all grain stored where your horse cannot get into it.

Do all diet changes gradually, including getting them used to a new lush pasture, or seasonal changes in the grass. Watch their weight in the spring when the grass is in bloom and rich. Your horse might not be able to be turned out as long each day, or another alternative is to substantially cut back on his grain if the grass is giving him enough. Also, keep up on your horse's trimming.

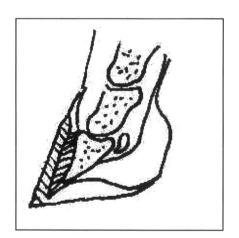 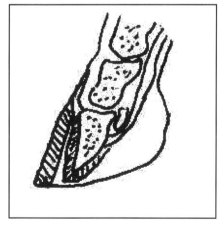

Moderate Laminitis   Severe Laminitis

Ringworm:

Description:
Ringworm is a fungal infection of your horse's skin that is contagious to other horses and to other animals (including humans). The main sign of ringworm is patchy hair loss without itching. (Mostly in a circular shape about the size of a nickel or quarter)

Treatment:
*   Clipping hair away from affected areas
*   Daily bathing with iodine-based shampoo
*   Application of antifungal ointments after each bath
*   Strict maintenance of dry shelter
*   Exposure to sunlight whenever possible
*   For severe cases, oral administration of anti-fungal medications may be necessary.

Rain Rot:

Description:
A crusting skin disorder affecting your horse's saddle area. The organism that causes has characteristics of both bacteria and fungi. It tends to appear in wet weather when the skin is waterlogged and less capable of fighting infection. It can be spread to other horses by contaminated grooming tools. You will see and feel tufts of crusted-together hair that is easily pulled out. When it is pulled out, there is a raw spot remaining on your horse's skin.

Treatment:
*   Softening the removal of scabs
*   Disinfection of affected area with iodine or chlorhexidine-based shampoos or rinses
*   Strict hygiene and provision dry shelter
*   Disinfection of grooming tools
*   Sever cases may also be treated with oral antibiotics

Wounds

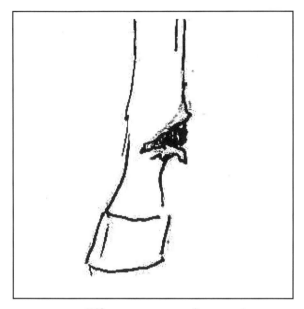

There are many different types of cuts. Some you can treat yourself and some require veterinarian care.

A minor flesh wound that has become swollen and warm might mean that it is infected, but mostly means that it is un-complicated swelling, heat, pain and discharge that are necessary components to heal. It could get infected though, so take care of it immediately.

Minor flesh wounds can be treated with correct cleaning and ointment application, and even bandaging.

Wounds that are deep (if you can pull the skin apart) need stitches. Keep the wound soft until your veterinarian arrives.

If you can see muscle, tendon or bone, call your veterinar-ian right away and keep your horse quiet and calm. Wounds like that, even after being healed, most often create permanent dam-age to the horse.

To prevent wounds, inspect your horse's stall and pasture regularly for sharp objects. Keep up on his shoeing so he does not pull off his shoe and cut himself. Try to keep horses that fight with each other separate. Even despite all your efforts, your horse is still prone to cuts. Still though, do your best to prevent them from happening.

First Aid Kit
Tools:
- Rectal thermometer
- Latex gloves
- Sharp Scissors
- Steel Cup or Container
- Stethoscope
- Chemical cold pack
- Electric clippers (#40 blade)
- Hoof pick
- Hoof knife
- Shoe pullers
- Hoof boots
- Combination pocket knife/tool kit
- Trigger-type spray bottles

Bandaging Materials:
- 1 lb rolls of fluffy cotton
- thick sanitary napkins
- disposable diapers
- Self Adhesive Bandaging (Vetrap)
- Gauze pads in assorted sizes
- Gauze Wrap (4 inch rolls of stretch gauze)
- Adhesive Wrap and Adhesive Tape
- Leg Wraps
- Duct Tape
- Bandage Scissors

Medications:
- Electrolyte Powder or paste.
- Dewormer

Cleansing and/or Debriding Agents:
- Saline Solution
- 10% benzoyl peroxide acne cleanser
- medicated scab softener (Corona®, silvadine)

Drawing Agents (Swelling):
- Poultice (Commercial bought or homemade)
- Saran Wrap
- Paper Towels

Disinfectants:
- Betadine® Solution
- Nolvasan® Solution
- Betadine® Scrub
- Emollient, Anti-Inflammatory, Anti-Itch, and Protecting

Agents:
- Non-antibiotic first aid cream, like zinc oxide, Corona ointment®, and 100% aloe vera gel.
- DMSO gel
- Cortison ointment
- Fly repellant for open wounds, such as Swat®
- Zinc oxide or titanium dioxide cream (Sunblock)
- Calamine lotion
- Petroleum jelly

Keep your first-aid kit current! There is nothing worse than not having what you need when your horse needs you most.

Section 5

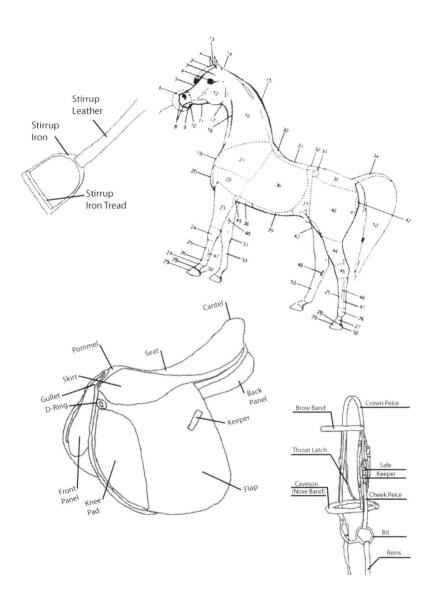

Stirrup Leather

Stirrup Iron

Stirrup Iron Tread

Cantel

Pommel

Seat

Skirt

Gullet

D-Ring

Back Panel

Keeper

Front Panel

Knee Pad

Flap

Brow Band

Crown Peice

Throat Latch

Safe

Keeper

Caveson (Nose Band)

Cheek Peice

Bit

Reins

Horse Terms

50 HORSE PARTS

1 - Ear
2 - Forelock
3 - Temple
4 - Eye
5 - Nose
6 - Notril
7 - Muzzle
8 - Lips
9 - Chin
10 - Chin Groove
11 - Branches of Jaw
12 - Cheek
13 - Optical Crest
14 - Poll
15 - Crest
16 - Neck
17 - Throatlatch
18 - Jugular Groove
19 - Point of Shoulder
20 - Chest
21 - Shoulder
22 - Upper Arm
23 - Forearm
24 - Knee
25 - Cannon
26 - Fetlock Joint
27 - Pastern

28 - Coronet
29 - Hoof
30 - Withers
31 - Back
32 - Loin
33 - Point of Hip
34 - Dock of Tail
35 - Croup
36 - Barrel (Ribs)
37 - Flank
38 - Brisket
39 - Belly
40 - Thigh
41 - Buttock
42 - Point of Buttock
43 - Stifle
44 - Gaskin
45 - Hock
46 - Suspensory Ligament
47 - Flexor Tendon
48 - Chestnut
49 - Elbow
50 - Heel
51 - Trapezium
52 - Tail
53 - Cannon Bone

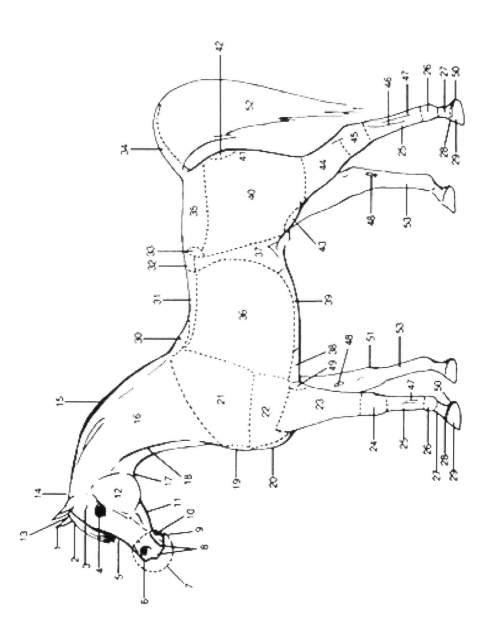

169

ENGLISH SADDLE PARTS

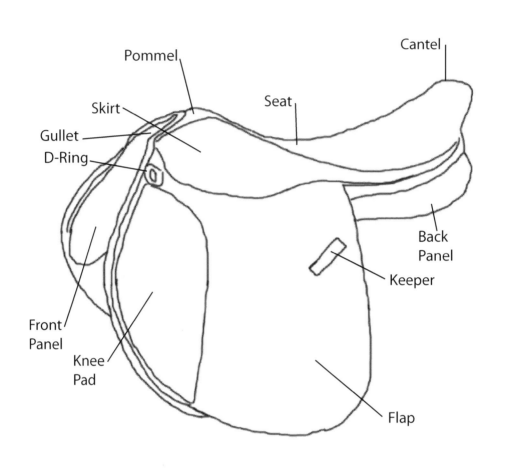

Pommel

Cantel

Skirt

Seat

Gullet

D-Ring

Back Panel

Keeper

Front Panel

Knee Pad

Flap

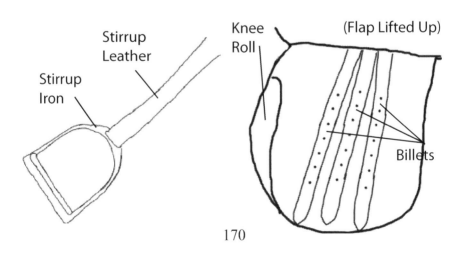

Stirrup Leather

Knee Roll

(Flap Lifted Up)

Stirrup Iron

Billets

170

DIFFERENT ENGLISH SADDLES

Hunter/Jumping
With or Without Knee Rolls,
Longer and Flatter Seat, Set
Forward Flaps for Short Stir-
rup Jumping Position

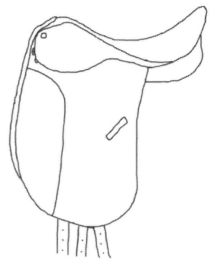

Dressage
Long Flaps, Deep Seat
Long Billets for Short Girth

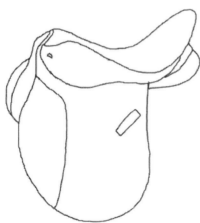

All Purpose
Made for both jumping and
dressage. Characteristics of
both saddles above com-
bined.

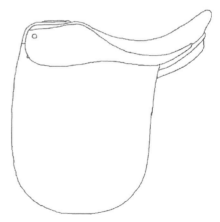

Cutback/Saddleseat
Longer and Flatter Seat,
Pommel cuts back deeper
for comfort for the laid back
shoulder and high set neck
horse.

ENGLISH BRIDLE PARTS

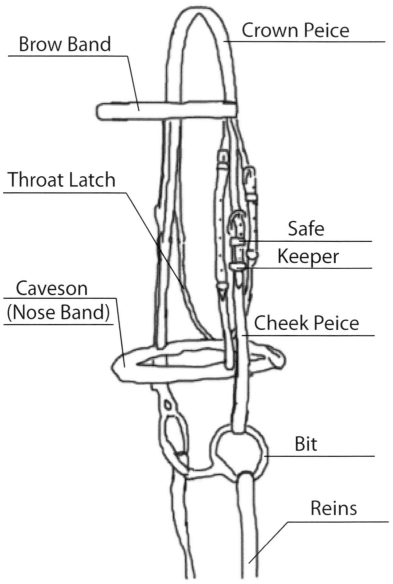

Crown Peice

Brow Band

Throat Latch

Safe
Keeper

Caveson
(Nose Band)

Cheek Peice

Bit

Reins

Crown Peice, Brow Band, Cheek Peices, Caveson and Throatlatch all together is called the HEADSTALL.

Western Tack

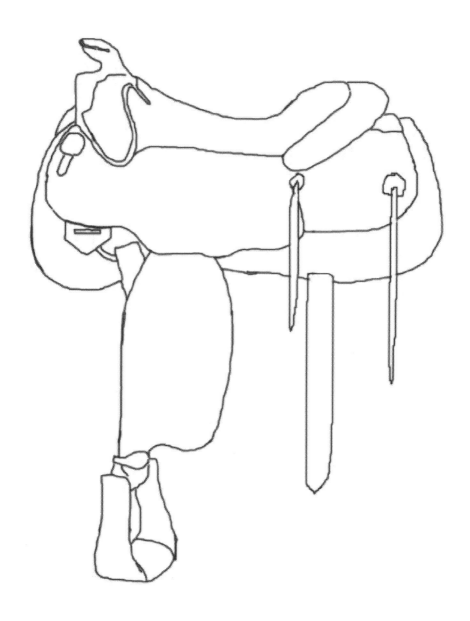

WESTERN SADDLE PARTS

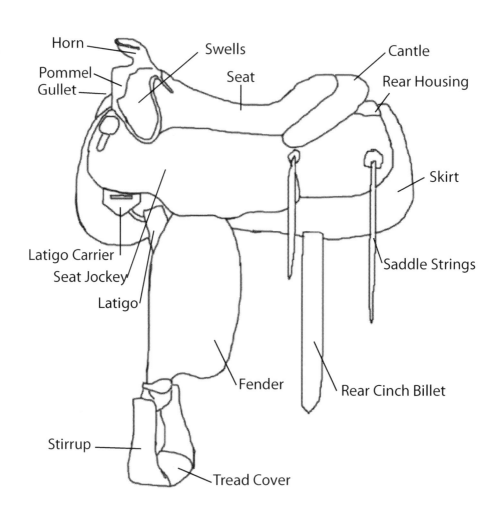

Horn

Pommel
Gullet

Swells

Seat

Cantle

Rear Housing

Skirt

Latigo Carrier

Seat Jockey

Latigo

Saddle Strings

Fender

Rear Cinch Billet

Stirrup

Tread Cover

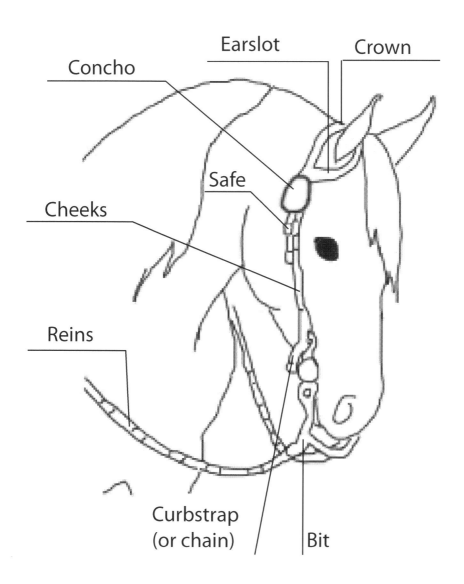

Earslot

Crown

Concho

Safe

Cheeks

Reins

Curbstrap
(or chain)

Bit

Face Markings

Star (In between eyes/on forehead)

Strip (between forhead and muzzle)

Snip (between nostrils on muzzle)

Upper Lip (there can also be marking on lower lip)

Blaze (wide marking from   Bald Face (wide marking
forehead to muzzle)   covering eyes and nostrils

Markings on the face can be all different sizes and shapes. You identify what they are called by where they are placed on the horse's face. These pictures demonstrate where the placings of each marking are.

Horses may have a combination of the markings on the previous page. For example, one horse could have a star, strip, snip, upper lip and lower lip. The "blaze" is actually a combination of star, strip and snip.

Some horses have no markings at all. As you can see, just like humans, no two horses ever look the exact same.

Leg Markings

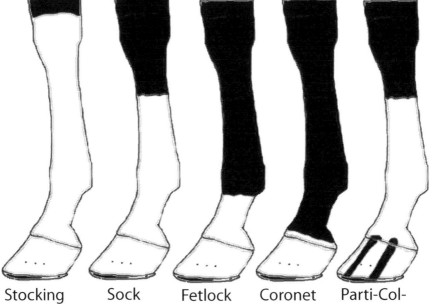

| Stocking (on knee or hock) | Sock (on cannon bone) | Fetlock (on or below fetlock joint) | Coronet (right around hoof) | Parti-Colored Hoof (spots of black on the coronet) |

Horse Colors

Bay

A bay horse is one who's coat is a shade of brown with BLACK POINTS. The points of the horse are its legs, tips of ears, muzzle, mane and tail. There are many different shades of a bay horse, but all have black legs, mane and tail. The other shades are known as: black-bay, dark bay, blood bay and light bay.

Chestnut

A chestnut horse is one who's coat is a shade of red (or closer to orange). The mane and tail are either exactly the same shade as the coat or just slightly darker and in some cases lighter, (just not black). When the mane and tail is lighter, or a shade of "blonde", it is called "flaxen".

Liver Chestnut

A liver chestnut horse is one who's coat is a deep chestnut, or a liver color, hence the name. Like lighter chestnut horses, the mane and tail are the same color or a couple shades darker.

Black

A true black horse does not have any brown anywhere on the coat or points, but is a deep black all over. If they do have brown in the coat, they would be considered a bay.

Grey (Steel, Dappled, Rose, Flea-Bitten)

A grey horse is one who's skin is black, and who's coat is white or grey. All grey horses have black skin, with the exception of "albino" horses, who have pink skin (but then they are not called greys). All grey horses are born a solid color (bay, chestnut or black) and turn white over the years. They will start to show around their eyes and muzzle as a foal and then white hairs will appear all throughout their coat until it "consumes" them.

"Steel grey" is a deep grey and is one of the first stages a lot of grey horses will go through. "Rose grey" is another stage that horses born chestnut will go through as they turn grey. "Dappled grey" is seen when spots or "dapples" appear on the body of the coat. Then, after the horses turn all white, (or sometimes even when they are still in the dapple grey stage) they will get brown or chestnut colored flecks throughout the coat and this is called "flea-bitten".

Palomino
The palamino color is a light golden coat with a white, or cream colored mane and tail. There are a couple different breeds that can be a palamino color.

Buckskin
Buckskin is a tan color horse with black legs, mane and tail and a dark dorsel stripe down the spine.

Paint (a breed)
A paint is either a Thoroughbred or a Quarter Horse that is white and a solid color in large markings around the body. So, a paint is actually a breed while a "pinto" (below) is a color.

Pinto
A pinto is the same coloring as a paint, but is a term given to other breeds other than a Thoroughbred or Quarter Horse.

Terminology

Genders

Mare: a female horse that is age 4 and over
Stallion: a male horse that is age 4 and over that is able to reproduce.
Gelding: a male horse that has been "gelded" (neutered) and is any age.
Colt: a male horse that has not been gelded and is age 3 and under
Filly: a female horse that is age 3 and under

OTHER:

Foal: a baby horse indicating both genders
Sire: the father of a foal
Dam: the mother of a foal

Veterinarian:
a doctor and physisian for animals
Farrier:
a person who trims and puts shoes on horse's hooves.

Section 6
Horsie Stories

Photo by Leslie Hodgson

Photo by Rachel Hamblin

Photo by Stuart Vesty

SRF Make Myne Mynk++/ "Mynk"
Half-Arabian Chestnut Mare
(Zodiac Matador x Jac Lu Mars Frolic, Saddlebred)

The first thing that comes to mind when Mynk's name is mentioned is how much heart she has. If my life was ever in the hands of one of my horses, Mynk would be the horse I'd choose.

I had the privilege of showing Mynk in H/A English Pleasure JOTR and JTR. Every time we entered the ring it was a new and exciting experience. Mynk puts her whole heart and soul into every show. At the little shows she got so hyped going down the runway that she felt like a speed boat. You know when they first take off their front end elevates so much you feel like you might fall out the back? That's what riding Mynk is like. When they call for that trot, you better be ready for it!

At Youth Nationals, Mynk never gave up. Through both the cuts she gave her all. Then for the final class, I asked for more, and she gave more. Willingness like that in a horse, a horse like Mynk,

184

brings tears to my eyes. Mynk and I went on to go Top Ten in both the classes!

At Canadian Nationals I was ready to give my all for the roses, I knew it would be Mynk's last National class. The first class was great, but the second class, her last class was the greatest experience of my life. I felt invincible on that horse. I could feel the... I can't even explain it. I guess I could explain it by saying, right there at that moment, mine and Mynk's hearts were one. Perfect Harmony! It was emotional and exciting.

The call judge called for the line up at the walk and the crowd started boo-ing. So she said we could trot in. At that opportunity Mynk and I gave it one last round. While in the line up, Mynk had her ears forward looking around at the crowd. She looked so content. I was holding back tears.

When we got called back in for our top ten ribbon, the crowd exploded. It was a great feeling. Again, for our Top Ten victory pass, the crowd's response was overwhelming, my tears were streaming during the whole thing. After I cleared the gait I jumped off and hugged my mom who was also in tears. Then we turned and hugged Mynk. What a great horse.

Mynk came home after that show and settled right in. She gave rides to people who always have dreamed of riding her. Having Mynk in the barn is almost magical. She loves being scratched and she always had tic tacs by her door. (She loves those!)

Then, Mynk did another great act, she gave birth to a beautiful bay filly on April 27th 2001. We named this filly "Make My Heart Sing LC", and that she does! We call her "Groovy". She is amazing. She is so much like her mother its almost spooky. Their presence, the lady-like manner in which they walk, the trot and snort and blow.. its all the same!

185

Mynk will always live with us. Even if we sell everyone else, Mynk will stay ours. At home Mynk has enjoyed trail rides, swimming in the river, and hours of sunny pasture time with her foals.

Mynk will be back in the show ring here and there. We owe it to her to let her hear the roaring crowds. She loves the show ring. The louder you scream for her, the higher she trots. So, if you ever see Mynk show, cheer for her... she'll give you a show you'll never forget.

WCF Reyna+/ "Reyna"
Half-Arabian Chestnut Mare
(Zodiac Matador x Sensational Wave, Saddlebred)

Reyna's story is an exciting one! It began on June 30, 1992 when a beautiful chestnut filly was born at Al and Sue Rainwater's Winners Circle Farm. Her dam was Sensational Wave, a bay Saddlebred mare who was well accomplished herself. Al & Sue bred Sensational Wave to Zodiac Matador, who needs no introduction, and the result was beautiful Reyna.

This filly grew up beautifully but was, for a while, a little difficult to train. But under the guidance of Michael Lamb at River Ridge Farm, Reyna began her unbelievable wins in Half Arabian Country English Pleasure.

In 1999 Reyna was named Region 4, Region 5, and Canadian Reserve National Champion, and US Top Ten with Sue Rainwater in the Amateur division. She was also Region 4 and Region 5 Champion, Canadian Reserve National Champion and US National Top Ten with Mike Lamb in the Open division.

We entered the picture in the fall of 2000. We purchased Reyna for Rachel to ride. Rachel by this time had earned her way to a horse of Reyna's caliber. Rachel had been on good and bad horses, but nothing the quality of which she was about to ride. Her previous step up the ladder was riding Starlin Afire to National Top Tens in purebred Country English Pleasure. Starlin is a great mare and taught Rachel all she needed to know about riding a big time show horse.

So, now we begin to tell you about the fairy tale season of 2001. Reyna loves Rachel, and Rachel is dedicated to Reyna. Normally, Reyna hates a lot of "traffic", and tails being swooshed in her face and the like. What we discovered at Scottsdale 2001, (their first show together), was that Reyna trusted Rachel and she took care of her. Those Junior Exhibitor Half Arabian Country English classes tend to be large! Not once in the ring did Reyna ever freak out if another horse was too close or if a tail was swooshed in front of her. When Rachel rides her, even at home, her ears are pricked forward and she goes around the ring perfectly content with her job.

Here is the show record for 2001 of this amazing duo:
Scottsdale Champion JOTR & JTR unanimous
Region IV Champion JOTR & JTR unanimous
Region V Champion JOTR unanimous
Youth National Reserve Champion JTR
Youth National Champion JOTR
Canadian National Champion JTR unanimous
Canadian National Champion JOTR

Making Reyna and Rachel Triple Crown Winners in JOTR!

Isn't that awesome!? They both highly deserve it. Reyna earned her Legion of Supreme Honor with these wins.

Prior to Scottsdale 2002, we received a box in the mail from IAHA. To our delight, it was a letter and a jacket. The jacket was embroidered "2001 IAHA Top Ten High Point Horse". The letter stated that Reyna was the #9 horse in the high point list for all horses enrolled in IAHA's Achievement Awards Program for 2001! Reyna earned 169 points in one year. The winner earned 279 points (all in dressage). So, Reyna was a Top Ten High Point Horse. She never ceases to amaze us.

Rachel and Reyna pulled it together one more time, again earning Championships at Scottsdale 2002. They were undefeated!

So, many might ask, what can we expect from this mare in the future? Your answer is simple; beautiful heirs to her throne from the breeding program of Amethyst Arabians, and many more show ring experiences!

Mares

Each mare is precious and holds a special place within my heart. Each morning when the door is rolled open I can recognize each of their delighted whinnies. I say "Good morning ladies!" and I am again answered with eager neighs. They show so much gratitude for what we give them. I too am pleased and feel comforted when alas I hear them happily munching their oats and hay. Going out to play is their next big event. The barn fills with anxious whinnies and stomping feet until you open the door with a halter in hand. To hear and watch them romp around the huge pastures, flipping their heads, bucking high and kicking out with wonderful excitement is highly entertaining and rewarding. My families farm is horse paradise and every horse is treated as royalty. When the sun begins to come down and the pastures are caressed in a soft sunlight, the herd of mares begin to make their journey to the gate. We greet each one of them with a halter and lead in hand whenever they are ready to come in. They are truly ladies, each behaving very well. Again, the sound of them happily eating brings a smile to my face, and I know I can sleep well.

If having just the mares is special, imagine when they have foals! To witness the love and bond between mother and foal is priceless above all other experiences. I love to see them nicker to each other and create a bonded relationship. And when mamma stands to lick her new born baby I get lost in thoughts of what she is thinking. Then as I look and smile at the foal while it is getting frustrated to find 'the faucet', images of the future start running through my mind. My thoughts wander to the many days they have to romp in the sunshine, then I ponder possibilities of each stage of its youth and even on into the future show ring. As I see what an awesome new creature stands proudly before me, I get eager with excitement and I have a hard time waiting for what the future holds So, until then, it is the mothers job to nurture and teach this young horse so it will be well behaved and know how to use that Arabian blood and characteristics to reach its full potential. Each of our great mares love their babies and especially enjoy showing them off to let the world see what a great and marvelous treasure they have created.

There is nothing more treasured to us than an Arabain mare. Her eyes that see your soul. Her lips that tickle your ears. Her tail carried high and proud. When you place your hand on her you feel a connection to her somehow. Her neck arched as a swan gliding over the water. Soft and gentle is her touch. She floats along the ground like an angle with wings. When she quietly stands and breathes very softly, I know that she understands all of my thoughts, sad and joyful. And she is dedicated to please us and to show us every day she is special. Truly, mares are a blessing from heaven.

Determination

I was in the blistering heat of Oklahoma City, sweating, sore and tired when my dream was fulfilled. My horse "Forgery" and I were entered in one of the toughest classes of "The Arabian and Half-Arabian Youth National Championship." Since the riding arena is only so big, and the judges can only see so many horses at one time, large classes are split into elimination classes. Sadly, some horses and riders must be eliminated from the competition to pick the final ten winners and then a champion. Forgery and I were in two different types of riding events, each with two elimination classes, and then the finals. So, together we had 6 performances. By the end of the week, Forgery and I had endured, performed well, and impressed the judges enough that they kept us in the qualifying classes to show in the finals.

Finally, the semifinal/final class had arrived. Forgery and I were both exhausted from the one hundred degree weather and the hard, repetitious work. It had been a long year. We showed in many qualifying regional competitions, learned much, traveled far, and made and fixed mistakes.

Trotting into the arena for the final performance, Forgery and I pulled together all the scarce energy we had, all the great memories we'd shared, and all the learning and bonding we had achieved, and showed the world what we were made of. Performing each transition and gait with style and determination we made it through the class. Now, the moment of truth had arrived. It was time to announce the Top Ten winners.

Before I move on, I want to give an idea of the process one goes through to reach the Top Ten. You start out in small 'class A' shows, and must get a first or second place. (That was back in that year, there is a new point system now). Then in Regional shows you must get a Top Five or better. In my particular division, there are about 70-85 horses throughout the Nation that qualify to even attend Nationals. There are 17 Regional Shows across the nation, each with about 3-5 horses qualifying out of a class of 6-15 horses. The total number of horses at a National Show is usually anywhere from one thousand to fifteen hundred horses. There are around one hundred different events or "classes". Each horse usually shows in one to two classes, but some horses do more divisions. In my class at the Nationals, (the Half Arabian Country English Pleasure JOTR (Junior Owner to Ride) ages 14-17) there were 55 horses to start. The three judges can only call back eight to twelve horses from each section cut. In this national show, the 55 horses were split up into three different sections and then the 8-12 horses and riders who received the honors to be seen again by the judges are split into two different sections.

Finally, the horses chosen from the two final sections (8-12 from both) are to be seen again in the finals. In the finals there are still around 16-24 horses. Now, after this performance, the judges' points are added up and the class is narrowed down to ten horses and riders. Much to my relief, my number was called and I received the great honor of being in the Top Ten of one of the largest classes in the show.

Next, out of the Top Ten, they pick two champions. First, the Reserve Champion, or the second place horse and rider is announced. Joy in the rider and in his or her family is strongly expressed through tears, smiles and hugs. The crowd applauds, pictures are taken with the red and white roses and a bronze colored trophy is presented. What an accomplishment! Second place!

Now the crowd hushes to hear the announcer give us the champion... the National Champion. Most announcers like to torture us by prolonging the suspense as long as possible and this one was no exception. Here I am listening to the announcer explain what a National Champion is, hoping, remembering all my daydreaming and my countless hours I have spent to one day win those red roses. I clue back in to hear the announcer say, "And our National Champion is (pause for dramatic affect)... Forgery DGL and Leslie Cook!"

Even now, as I sit here writing this I am stumped as to what to say next, because it is so hard to explain what I felt at that moment. Mostly, I was shocked. When you spend your whole life working towards just one moment in time, and it is finally there... what do you do? Well, I smiled. I did not want the moment to ever pass, and I wish I could still be in it at this moment. The felling of victory had overcome me and all I could do was say "thank you!" My hands had begun to shake due to the adrenaline rush of extreme excitement. I probably felt close to how the newly announced Miss America feels when they are placing the crown on her head and handing her roses.

Living my dream, I trotted forward to receive my blanket of roses, the moment unfolding as I had so often envisioned. Then I gazed at the trophy that I imagined would one day be shining on my shelf in my room where I could see it every day. I was soon joined in the arena by my trainer and my parents for a picture to capture the moment that we had all put so much time and effort into. Winning Nationals takes a team, and I am so grateful for my trainer and especially for my parents!

You can bet that all the tears, sweat, blood, sleep deprivation, and greasy horse show food were all beyond worth it. The fact is, I didn't even think of the struggle. All I thought about was how sweet my victory was. Not only did it happen once, but Forgery and I were crowned champion twice. Two times... can you believe it? I couldn't.

I want to back up to the time when Nationals, or winning at the Nationals, was just a goal or a dream of mine. Obviously to go anywhere that big and to spend that much money, you need support. One day, I told my dad I wanted to go to Nationals. He said, "OK, so what do you have to do to get there?"

My answer came quickly, "I have to practice really hard, long hours so I can qualify at the "Class A' shows to get to Regionals. Then qualify at Regionals to get to Nationals." He said that he wanted me to put it in writing and then determine if I was willing to pay the price—not only to go, but to win.

Along with my desire to go, came a lot of thinking on my part of what I had to give up so I could spend all the time I could in preparation to show, and win at the national level. These sacrifices included the time I could have spent having fun with my good friends who were outside the "horse world", and vacations my family could have taken. Most of all I sacrificed all of my time and energy. Horses are powerful, but helpless animals. To tend them is a full time job. Also, to get to the training barn where my horse stands requires traveling for close to an hour. On average I spend about 60 hours a week with all my horses. Also, sleep is among one of the greatest sacrifices a teenage girl can make, and this too, I gave up in large quantities.

There is a popular movie that I like to consider a classic.

It is titled, A League of Their Own". There is a scene in it that can lift me when I start to think it is all getting too hard, and I recall it often. Dotty Hensen (Geena Davis) has decided to leave the Woman's All American Baseball League after her husband, injured, returns from the war. When the coach, Jimmy Dugan (Tom Hanks) sees her not boarding the bus with the team, he goes over and begins to speak with her. As the conversation progresses she states, "Look! It just got to hard!" Then Mr. Dugan relies to her, "Of course it's hard. It's supposed to be hard. If it wasn't hard everyone would do it! The hard is what makes it great."

This is true with everything challenging that you choose to embark upon. "If it wasn't hard everyone would do it. The hard is what makes it great."

The journey to becoming a National Champion was hard. The harder it got, I found myself faced with more of a challenge. Though, if you know me, you would know that I love rising to a challenge... it thrills me. Without a challenge it becomes easy, therefore in my eyes, it exceeds being boring.

What made it easy for me to sacrifice other important things, and to fight the challenge is that I had a passion for the sport and a strong desire to get what I wanted. I am very strong headed. The things I had to sacrifice and the challenges I faced made me question my desire to carry out and fulfill my dreams. I wondered if I really had what it took to stick with it. I would soon remember though, that anything worth achieving is worth fighting for. If something you love and want is so important to you, you should be willing to sacrifice whatever you can, and do whatever it takes. If it is worth achieving, it is worth all the strength you can give it. The victory is always more sweet when you have to climb a mountain to get there.

This I learned through my accomplishments of a dream I once had. I still continue to dream. There are many more mountains I want to climb, and life is abundant of victories to be won. If I continue to dream, then I must continue improving and persevering.

I hope you find, as I am finding that in all aspects of life, from business to hobbies, from education to a career, and from family and friends, that there will be many challenges and a tough journey that you will have to face. I hope you remember that if it wasn't hard, everyone would do it. I hope you realize that anything worth having in your life is worth giving your might and your power until you have attained it. Keep your eye on your goal and never give up on your dreams. Victory is sweet.

Lessons from Big Red
Blog Written by Leslie October 9, 2010

Maybe I am only saying this because I'm a "horse girl", but maybe it's true too, but I think Secretariat, the movie that just came out was one of the best and inspirational movies of all time. And clean. I understand most of you that read this blog will not have seen it yet, might not see it in a while, or never. But quickly, here are a few lessons from the movie.

REJOICE IN OTHERS SUCCESSES

In the movie is casted "Ogden Phipps", who was then the "richest man in the world". He and the Chenerys were to have a coin toss for the choice between one of two foals out of the Chenery's mares, by Phipps' Stallion. Long story short, Phipps got the one he wanted but it turned out to be a horse that "his accountants could outrun", while Miss Chenery got Secretariat (the one she wanted). Most people would cut all ties to "the horse they lost" in a stubborn affirmation. Mr. Phipps however lead the investors in the Secretariat Syndicate, and was there at the races cheering him on and congratulating his owner.

How often to we, as humans, think that there is not enough success to go around? Ogden Phipps attitude of rejoicing with others in their successes is WHY he is successful, because he doesn't have any fears that others will "take up" the amount of success there is to be had.

Be honestly happy for people. Not to get "buddy-buddy" with them to "get a piece", but to honestly celebrate with them and for them . . . because the law of abundance states "there is enough for everybody", AND THERE IS!

"I'M GOING TO BEAT YOU"

Have you ever noticed that the politicians who spend their time trying to bring down their opponent often loses, while the one who was focused on campaigning their views or whatever wins? I'm not saying this is ALWAYS true, and I am not saying that the politician that focused on their campaign are pure or anything, just that the person who focuses on bringing somebody else down gets brought down themself.

I've learned this at horse shows too. I watched trainers or any rider for that matter who knew which horse was likely to win spend the entire class trying to "cover him up" from the judges sights. And it never really stopped that horse from winning anyway. That horse still wins and they just lost the opportunity to make their own horse perform its best for the judges.

The owner of "Sham", who was Secretariat's rival, acted just like that. All he talked about was "bringing Secretariat down". Well, he got what he was focused on didn't he? The law of attraction responds to negative words. He was talking about bringing down, he got brought down.

TRAIN HARD

After Secretariat had won the first two legs of the triple crown, the owner and trainer had a talk about what to do with him in the 2 or 3 weeks to the Belmont, which was the longest race of the three. A mile and a half. The trainer's instinct was to train him hard, though most owners rest their horses. Their fear of "ruining" Secretariat was strong. But that was their instinct, and they went with it. I would have done the same thing. The horse needs to be fit! He had the heart and the willpower to handle it, and the owner and trainer knew that, even though his "bone chips" and other concerns suggested maybe they should rest him.

Sham's owner decided they would rest theirs. To get straight to the point, Secretariat won the last race in the triple crown by

THIRTY-ONE lengths, and his time (speed) or furlongs in which he won has never been even approached.

Try hard, train hard, get fit, and you'll be ready for anything. And of course, the whole message of the movie from Miss Chenery's vigilant attitude is: DON'T GIVE UP and DON'T TAKE NO FOR AN ANSWER. These are common themes with anybody successful. Like J.K. Rowling who received about a dozen rejections of Harry Potter before someone published it. Miss Chenery (actually Mrs. Tweedy) NEVER took no for an answer and in the end, she saved her family and her farm. She didn't let impossible odds stopping her from achieving what she knew could happen. In this is another lesson: FOLLOW YOUR GUT! We are all blessed with the ability to judge and discern. Use it, listen to it, and don't let nay-sayers bring you down and change your mind.

My mom did this once with a horse we were going to sell, who we bought for a LOT. My mom won two Reserve National Championships with her, and after that, trainers were trying to tell us she was "just a broodmare" who was only worth $20,000 or $25,000. She (Song is the horse's name), never won even a Top Ten at Nationals in the Open Division. My mom told the trainers, similarly to how Secretariat's owner talked, "She is NOT just a broodmare, and she's worth more money."

Later, we sold Song for around $50,000 (I'll have to check with my mom exactly), and guess what? She went on to WIN that Top Ten in the Open Division of mare halter at Nationals, and they sold her for even MORE. My mom's instincts were always right, and it's a good thing that we often "ignored" trainers.

Well, that's about all. The movie was amazing. I'll see it again and again. I need the type of inspiration that will make me work (train) harder and not give up. Thank you for reading my little "lessons", and I hope you gained some inspiration for your life.

MY FAVORITE PLACE TO NAP

(Writen by Leslie 08/20/09
for an Assignment for her Writing School)

The cement isle of the horse barn held onto the coolness of the night, and always lasted through the fiery hot days. Flies would hit the shady coolness and bounce away from it like it had stung them. Inside the barn, comfortably munching his hay stood my horse Casanova. The silvery-white sight of his coat always transported me to a fantasy world, and I expected to see a Unicorn's horn on his forehead.

I placed my hand on the cool metal of his door handle, and rolled open the big wooden door, quickly closing it behind me again, so that I was hidden inside the stall with him. He took a few steps towards me and I placed one hand on his silky-smooth neck, and felt his warm-breath on my other hand. After a long, emotional day I wrapped my arms around his neck and drank in the tonic to my troubles: the smell of his sun-baked mane and lingering citronella in the fly spray.

I wanted to stay in that cedar-bedded stall for a lot longer with him so I gently pressed my fingers into his shoulder, and he pivoted into the center of the stall. I laced my fingers into the sturdy strands of his mane, stepped back until my arms were stretched straight, and then skip-jumped and in a flash had my leg up and over his back. Casanova let out a little snort but kept his feet firmly balanced on the ground. I said sweet things to him with a gentle tone and he instantly relaxed and moved back over to his hay.

Carefully concentrating on my balance, I lifted my leg up and over his neck and was then sitting sideways like he was a bench. I had one more turn to go so I lifted the other leg up and over his rump, which now meant I was facing backwards. It's a weird sort of sensation, sitting backwards on a horse—there's really nothing in front of you to reach out and grab should a predicament present itself, but I trusted my faithful white horse.

In that refreshingly cool and fly-free stall, I laid my head down on his rump like it was the comfiest pillow imaginable and let my arms dangle down by his flanks. I took in a deep breath of that horsey-smell I wished I could bottle as perfume for horse-crazy girls, and exhaled all my worries away. I began to drift off to sleep listening to familiar sounds like the scratch-scratching of a straw broom on cement and the distant hum of the tractor at work. Casanova consistently munched his hay, and my contentment soon matched his and I was fast asleep like an angel on a cloud.

Another Book by Leslie Hodgson

Earth's scientists say stars are burning balls of gases—but what if what we see is just a veil to hide what is truly there? There are numerous worlds in our Universe and in the realm of the twelve Zodiac Constellations, the dictator Gershon has overpowered the true ruler of the Zodiacs and he wants all in the royal line killed.

Hidden on Earth from him are two teenage siblings, Stella and Isaac. They have had a very unique life on Earth, but don't know they are out of the ordinary until a series of mysterious, tragic and exciting events open their minds to the real Universe they live in, who they are, and that they have the powers to possibly free the Zodians.

Isaac and Stella are caught in a whirlwind of events both tragic and exciting as they travel the Universe and team with creatures from Constellations such as Pegasus and Draco to help protect them from Gershon who is fiercely hunting them.

Shooting Stars is refreshing fantasy that will keep readers turning the pages as they encounter a new kind of magic, the possibilities the Universe holds, escape, animal companionship, self-discovery and budding relationships.

You'll find it all in refreshing uniqueness!
• Mythical Creatures
• New Worlds
• Young, Budding Relationships
• Adventure and Escape
• Page Turning Suspense
• Coming of Age
• Self-Discovery

What readers are saying about Shooting Stars and Leslie Hodgson:

"Shooting Stars by Leslie Hodgson wasn't anything like I thought it would be. I was expecting some sci-fi type novel. Instead I was pleasantly surprised to find what I would consider a fantasy novel. When I began reading I was immediately drawn in by the action and the characters. Stella was a very realistic teenage girl who isn't so sure of herself and needed constant reassurance. Issac was the typical teenage boy, thinking he can do anything. I enjoyed the relationship between the siblings and the bond that they shared. Added into their lives were mythical creatures like winged horses and dragons! I loved the twists and turns that came at every corner. This novel was so full of action and the unexpected that I could not set it down! Overall this book is a great read! I was sad at the ending, I felt that it ended rather abruptly. I hope that means that there is another novel in the works to wrap up all of the loose ends. If so, I will be reading it!" - BookWorm

"Shooting Stars was a delightful read. The characters are distinct and lively, and the plot very intriguing. The end of each chapter always left me hungry for more. The magical world Hodgson created is well thought out, with tons of creative surprises. The book is clean, and filled with excellent values. I am looking forward to reading more from this talented author!" - Tasha F.

A Kid's Review
"The best book I've read in a long time! It was truly a good book. I liked that there were so many amazing creatures that all worked together to defeat evil! It was very interesting and full of detail and action. I strongly recommend this book to anyone who wants to have an exciting adventure!! Great for young adults!" - Meghan K.

CHAPTER 13

"Be aware that as you feel good, you are powerfully attracting more good things to you."

Stella

The stomping on the stairs didn't startle Stella too much. Since she had arrived at the lighthouse, she had been hovering in the in-between of sleep and awake. She slowly got out of bed, taking her blanket with her and made her way over to the gold button. Soon Maximus was standing in front of her at the bottom of the stairs.

"No shoes again today?" she asked with a sassy-pants smile.

Maximus looked at his feet, wiggled his toes and said, "The sand is cool and soft this morning. Will you join me for a walk right now? I need to speak with you."

"Am I in trouble?"

He smiled, "No, no . . . I actually need to show you something on the beach . . . a gift for you."

"A gift?" she asked.

Again Maximus smiled and nodded. Stella noticed he looked very tired this morning.

"I'll be right there, just let me change." she said.

"Wonderful," he said, turning back up the stairs to leave. "See you outside in a moment."

Stella hurriedly dressed, leaving her shoes off and rushed to meet Maximus outside.

"This way," he said and she joined him and together they set out on the beach.

Maximus said, "I know you have been through much this week Miss Stella."

Stella liked when he called her that, like she was an adult worthy of respect but at the same time a child worthy of his protection.

He continued, "I hate to burden you with more, but there is still much you must know."

She took in a breath and held it, glancing sideways at him. He returned her glance and then placed an arm around her shoulders, pulling her in tight next to his side as they continued to walk.

"I know the things I've been telling you are extraordinary and hard to believe. I also know you've been down on yourself."

She was embarrassed that Maximus perceived so much about her.

"I want to see you happy," he said as he turned them up the beach and started to walk toward the trees, "I needed to find something to help you be happy, for the weeks ahead are not going to get easier."

She had no idea what he could be referring to, but her stomach clenched all the same.

"Which is why I am glad I came into your room and saw the mural on your wall last night," he said.

Completely confused now, she looked up at him.

"You have seen a few things this week you haven't ever before seen. Last night, I went on a journey with you in mind, and I am about to show you something you've also never before seen, which I brought back for you. He is here for you. To help you."

At the word 'he', Stella's bewilderment grew exponentially. Before she could do so much as squeak a response, Maximus turned her and gently pushed her through the trees.

She was suddenly rooted to the spot, for there stood her dream. Looking back at her was a winged horse. She felt drawn forward to him and looked over at Maximus for permission as she started walking toward the horse. She received an encouraging nod and smile from him. She turned again to the horse, and as she did, he started walking to her as well.

Her heart was racing, and was also filling up with warmth and spilled onto her cheek in the form of a tear. This tear didn't bother her like sad, cold tears did. She was purely ecstatic. Her life's dream—the fantasy she always let run freely in her mind—this horse . . . she felt more fulfilled and happy than she could remember feeling in a long time.

They reached each other and Stella outstretched her hand, and the horse met it with his forehead. She stared unblinking at his red, glistening coat and his multi-colored golden mane and wings and she ran her fingers through his forelock. He softly closed his eyes.

His back was about level with the top of her head. His neck was muscular and formed a perfect arch like a swan. His ears were set upon the arching neck and noble head, pointing up and slightly forward like the horn of a unicorn. His body was thick in stature, but beautifully refined by his powerful muscles and thin, soft skin.

206

She ran her hand over his eye, down the curve of his neck, over the muscles on his shoulders and tentatively to the captivating feathers of his wings. They felt just like a bird's, but were larger and longer than on any bird she could remember seeing. They compressed under her strokes, and then again looked untouched as her hand moved past them.

The horse never moved while she moved around him, except to turn his head slightly and keep her in his sight. She heard Maximus walk up behind her and she spun around and wrapped her arms around his waist and hugged him. Maximus sighed deeply and patted her on the back, then said, "You will never know how much pain has been lifted off my heart to see the pain lifted off yours."

She stepped back from him so she could see his face. Somewhat unable to speak still, she stammered, "Thank . . . Maximus . . . he's . . . I can't . . . I don't . . ."

He hugged her, drawing her into him again, "You're welcome. I've received all the thanks I need just by seeing some sparkle return to your eyes. Your resemblance to your parents at this moment is startling."

This made a few more warm tears spill onto her cheeks. She felt closer and more connected to her parents at this moment for reasons she could not explain. "He's magical," she said and she turned around to face the horse again. He was still standing quiet and noble, gazing at her intently, "Does he have a name?" she asked.

"Let's let him introduce himself," replied Maximus.

Stella's head whipped to Maximus again, and then just as quickly back to the winged horse, because she heard him speak! "My name is Arrow, my lady," he said, in the language her parents had taught her.

Her mouth again was wide open, but no sound escaped her. Maximus laughed his deep, man's laugh, and walked over to stand next to Arrow. "Yes, he talks too," he said. "When a creature is intelligent like this, we capitalize their species. He is a Winged Horse, with a capital 'w' and 'h'. Let him tell you his story—you'll be simply amazed. Arrow, where are you from?"

"From Markab, on Pegasus," he said considerately and quietly toward Stella, probably trying to soften the effects of a talking Horse.

"That's the Constellation Pegasus," Maximus added when Stella looked at him, "Just like you are from Vega on the constellation Lyra, Arrow is from Markab on the constellation Pegasus."

"How did you get here?" she asked.

Maximus answered for Arrow, "In the same way as I have mentioned to you before—as a Star, which is the same way in which you saw your dad streaking across the sky, the same way your mother sent you here. We, meaning you, Isaac and I have the ability to change our molecular density to transform ourselves into stars, focus our minds, and arrive where we intend."

Stella knew Maximus was not trying to be insensitive, but she still didn't like mention of the night her parents died. Deciding not to react, she asked, still struggling to form coherent sentences, "I've . . . never . . . are you sure?"

"Yes, I am sure Stella. This is how I went to Pegasus just last night and returned with Arrow before you awoke."

Though it was beyond anything Stella had ever before even fathomed being possible, she knew it had to be true. Nowhere on Earth did there exist a horse with wings.

With the unexplained new connection she now felt to her parents, she now understood much, like why as a family they studied the stars daily. Just one thing still troubled her, every time this subject came up, "Why was all this kept a secret from Isaac and me?" Some of the hurt and confusion that so quickly fled when she saw Arrow was creeping back.

Arrow stepped to her and put his head down at the level of her torso. Again, it felt like some sort of magic to Stella—he emanated comfort like he had a direct line to her heart from which to feed his supply of confidence.

Maximus quietly said, "Why don't you take some time to get to know Arrow, and I will go bring your brother down to meet him and then talk with you both more about that."

"Sounds good," Stella said. She was again entirely engrossed in Arrow's majesty.

Maximus turned and left. When he was gone, Arrow knelt down and spread his left wing forward. Then he said to her, "Let me carry you for a while."

Mesmerized, Stella walked up to his back behind his wing and put her leg over. He stood up and she was sitting on his back. As he started walking forward, the excitement grew all the more within her. She noted to herself how he put much thought and care into each step he took. She didn't know what she should say to him, so she contented herself by looking at his neck as it subtly bobbed up and down as he walked.

His mane was like golden waves. His wings enveloped her legs like they had been made solely to shield her.

She dangled her legs casually, not feeling the need to grasp anything with her hands to stay on. She felt as if she'd been riding a Winged Horse her entire life.

It was Arrow who broke the silence between them, "Have you ridden on a Horse's back before? You feel very relaxed and balanced."

"No," she said simply, "you are the first Horse I've ridden."

"Hmmm…" he responded, "Maybe natural Horsemanship runs in your blood from your father."

"What do you mean? My father . . . did you know him?"

"Yes. He came to Pegasus several times—and he formed a very special bond with my sister, Zordosa."

"You mean, my father has been to your Star?" Stella felt a mix of thrill and again confusion as to why her parents did not share all these wonderful things about their lives.

"Oh yes, very often. His visits were not for any royal or political purpose. He liked to come just to be with the Horses. The bond he and my sister shared was a beautiful masterpiece."

Stella thought in silence. Arrow's hooves rhythmically ticked away the time as Stella was consumed in her own thoughts. Stella thought of her father riding a Winged Horse—as his favorite hobby. He probably was secretly proud of her almost obsessive interest in Horses. And maybe, she thought, he hated not sharing his secret of his friendship with Winged Horses with her.

Deep in thought, it took Stella a moment to realize that they were no longer on the soft ground of the treed area. Only when she found herself squinting in the sunlight and noticed the different feeling of Arrow's stride as he walked through the sand, did she know they were on the beach. She sighed just as she felt Arrow's ribcage expand widely under her and then heard him exhale with a gentle rattling noise from his nostrils.

She giggled and said, "Jinx!"

Arrow turned his head slightly so one of his eyes was more visible to her then said, "What does 'jinx' mean?"

"It means we both did or said something at the same exact time, and since I was the one that said 'jinx', you can't speak until I un-jinx you."

"But I am not finding it difficult to speak at all," he said cocking his nose to the side in obvious confusion.

209

Stella laughed aloud again, "It's just a game."

"Oh, I see. Well, I shall be silent then until you un-jinx me for sighing at the same time as you."

Stella stroked his neck. Even though it was a childish game, and he was a Horse after all, it still felt good to be so light-hearted and 'childish'.

Stella looked down the beach and wondered what it would be like to go faster. As if responding to her thoughts, Arrow gently moved into a slow trot. At this increased speed, she felt more comfortable holding his mane with her hands, but kept her body relaxed. Relaxed as she was, she felt that her body melded into Arrow's back as she absorbed all the motion.

Apparently satisfied she would not bounce off, Arrow increased his speed, and Stella's smile spread further across her face. Before his trot got too fast and bumpy, he transitioned into a smooth-as-glass canter. As he did this, they had reached the edge of the water.

Stella loved the rocking motion of the canter and felt so secure that she let go of his mane and extended her arms out like wings. To complete the feeling she was flying, she closed her eyes. Her hair was flowing and whipping behind her head like the flame on a fire. She felt weightless and deep in her imagination, she could even hear the flapping of wings.

Or was it her imagination? Stella opened her eyes. Arrow's hooves were no longer padding the beach. Instead, Stella found they were a few feet above the water—Arrow's wings spread out wide and gently flapping the salty air.

She quickly grasped large handfuls of Arrow's mane and clenched her legs and feet together against Arrow's sides. She no longer felt safe sitting up straight so she hunched over to be closer to Arrow and not lose her balance. None of these measures helped at all. She found it even more frightening and difficult to stay on, for she started slipping to the side despite the extra-firm grip she had on her Horse.

Arrow spoke a little louder than normal to be heard above the noise of the ocean and sea air as they flew through it, "Stella! You must relax as you were before!"

"I can't! I'll fall!"

"No, you won't! You'll fall if you do not relax. Close your eyes again and pretend like we are on the beach cantering."

"I don't want to."

"If you don't, we'll never be able to fly together. Don't you want to be able to fly?"

Stella hunched over a little farther and clenched a little tighter. "I just... I think I'll fall!"

"You won't. Just trust me!"

The thing she felt most comfortable doing first was to un-hunch her back and sit up straight. Doing this gave her an instant feeling of freedom and control over the situation.

"That's right!" said Arrow.

She could not stop the smile which began its reappearance at the corners of her mouth. She was slowly letting her legs relax and reveled in each sensation—the wind making her hair flow out behind her, the feel of Arrow's muscles moving under her legs as his wings moved up and down, the edge of his mane tickling her chin as it flowed back toward her.

She looked up in between his ears and saw the expanse of the beach in front of them, spreading on and curving around to disappear around the other side of the island. The speed at which they were passing over the waters exhilarating.

She felt Arrow lean to the side and turn so her view from between his ears changed from sand and ocean to purely ocean. She gripped Arrow's mane tighter, but willed herself to stay upright with relaxed legs and she let her body lean with the turn. Arrow completed the turn and then she saw the beach with the lighthouse.

"Much better!" she heard Arrow say over the rush of the wind.
She felt as if they truly were melding together and becoming a single being. He lowered his head and changed the angle of his wings, and they descended to the beach. He landed in a canter then slowed to a walk as he folded his wings around her legs.

"Hey!" she said suddenly remembering something. She slapped him playfully on the neck, "I never un-jinxed you!" They both laughed. Stella was delighted by the sound of his laugh—a wonderful mixture of laughter and neighing.

How she wished she would never have to leave Arrow's side. Now that they had landed, she instantly wanted to do it again and be up in the air . . . flying. Flying! She couldn't believe she had just flown . . . on a Horse's back . . . over the ocean.

Where to find more of Leslie and more of Harmony with Horses:

www.harmony-with-horses.com

www.lesliehodgson.com

www.shootingstarssaddleclub.com

"Like" Our Pages:
www.facebook.com/shootingstarssaddleclub

www.facebook.com/shootingstarsbook

44448518R00121

Made in the USA
San Bernardino, CA
15 January 2017